Line managers and family-friendly employment

Roles and perspectives

Sue Yeandle, Judith Phillips, Fiona Scheibl, Andrea Wigfield and Sarah Wise

The POLICY PRESS

First published in Great Britain in November 2003 by

The Policy Press
Fourth Floor, Beacon House
Queen's Road
Bristol BS8 1QU
UK

Tel no +44 (0)117 331 4054
Fax no +44 (0)117 331 4093
E-mail tpp-info@bristol.ac.uk
www.policypress.org.uk

© Sheffield Hallam University 2003

Published for the Joseph Rowntree Foundation by The Policy Press

ISBN 1 86134 556 9

Sue Yeandle is Professor of Sociology and Head of the Centre for Research in Social Inclusion at Sheffield Hallam University. **Judith Phillips** is Professor of Social Gerontology at the University of Keele. **Fiona Scheibl** is Research Fellow in the Health Services Research Unit at the London School of Hygiene and Tropical Medicine. **Andrea Wigfield** is a Senior Research Fellow in the Department of Sociological Studies at the University of Sheffield. **Sarah Wise** is a Research Associate at the Employment Research Institute, Napier Univeristy Business School, Edinburgh.

The **Joseph Rowntree Foundation** has supported this project as part of its programme of research and innovative development projects, which it hopes will be of value to policy makers, practitioners and service users. The facts presented and views expressed in this report are, however, those of the authors and not necessarily those of the Foundation.

The statements and opinions contained within this publication are solely those of the authors and not of The University of Bristol or The Policy Press. The University of Bristol and The Policy Press disclaim responsibility for any injury to persons or property resulting from any material published in this publication.

The Policy Press works to counter discrimination on grounds of gender, race, disability, age and sexuality.

Cover design by Qube Design Associates, Bristol
Printed in Great Britain by Hobbs the Printers Ltd, Southampton

Contents

Acknowledgements

The authors are grateful to their co-authors in the original studies for their work in producing the original data on which this study is based. They are: Miriam Bernard, Sue Bond, Minda Chittenden, Rosemary Crompton, Jane Dennett, Jeff Hyman and Juliette Summers. The authors would also like to thank the Joseph Rowntree Foundation, and especially Barbara Ballard and Shirley Dex, for financial support, very helpful comments and general encouragement in the development of this study.

Introduction

In the past decade, considerable attention has been given, in academic, professional and popular literature, to the need for employers to become more 'family-friendly', and to support their employees in developing a better 'work–life balance'. This report focuses on one key element in the set of processes which are now operating in many workplaces to achieve this: the role of the line manager. As is well established, simply having such policies in place does not resolve the many issues that arise when, in real and everyday situations, employees and managers try to implement them. This report is about the implementation of such policies, as described by managers with the day-to-day responsibility of dealing with staff needs and requests, alongside their additional and – in the view of some – their primary obligation to meet the operational and business requirements of their organisation.

The report brings together research data from four projects funded by the Joseph Rowntree Foundation within its 'Work and Family Life' programme. The four projects were conducted between 2000 and 2002 at five Universities: Cambridge, Keele, Napier, and Sheffield Hallam (in a joint project with City University). Details of the four studies are given in Appendix A. The idea for additional, secondary analysis of the face-to-face qualitative interviews with the line managers interviewed in each of these projects emerged at a meeting of the 'Work and Family Life' programme research teams. It was subsequently agreed that the four teams would pool this aspect of their data in a collaborative project designed to explore line managers' experiences of, beliefs about and attitudes towards the implementation of family-friendly policies and other organisational efforts to improve work–life balance.

Aims and objectives of the study

The main aim of the study was to provide additional analysis on how line managers implement flexible, family-friendly and carer-friendly policies, and to identify some of the factors which influence the way they behave when carrying out their roles as line managers. In particular, by creating a sample of line managers in 20 organisational settings, this analysis has attempted to answer the following research questions:

- How far do line managers' personal characteristics structure their attitudes and behaviour in implementing policies?
- What is the impact of factors such as staffing levels, staff turnover, and the type of work being managed?
- How aware are managers of the policies in place, and how does this affect the line manager's role?
- What impact does the wider ethos and culture of the organisation have on managers' implementation of flexible working policies?

The four research studies used as the basis for this report produced a total of 91 face-to-face interviews with line managers in the organisations selected for each study. This represents a substantial basis of data about line managers, but should not be taken as in any sense representative of the total population of UK line managers, or of UK organisations. In this chapter we summarise information about these managers' jobs, circumstances and responsibilities, as provided in the original interviews. This gives context, and enables us to relate the particular issues identified by managers in the study to particular types of work or organisation. It should also be remembered that the studies were not originally designed to be analysed together, and that there are consequently some differences in the data available in each case.

The managers

The 91 managers were drawn from 10 different large organisations and nine small and medium-sized enterprises (SMEs). Table 1.1 shows their gender and detailed distribution across the organisations.

Most of the managers (68 of the 86 for whom these data are available) had some personal experience of family and caring responsibilities – although not all of this was current. Table 1.2 shows these responsibilities at the time they were interviewed. Although almost all the managers were asked about their current family responsibilities, only a minority were questioned about past caring and parental roles.

As Table 1.2 shows, many of the managers in the SMEs and in financial services had current childcare responsibilities of their own, although it should be noted that in financial services, 15 of the 39 managers had no current care responsibilities at all. Few of the health service managers had current caring responsibilities of any kind, and none had dependent children to take care of at the time of the interviews.

Of course the distribution of the managers' caring responsibilities is linked to their ages. The managers interviewed in the SMEs were mostly aged 35-45, the prime childrearing years. In the local authorities and in the NHS trust the managers were mostly older, with many in their upper forties or fifties. The supermarket managers were the youngest group: seven of the nine managers here were under the age of 35, including some in their early twenties. The ages of the financial services managers were not known.

Table 1.1: Managers interviewed, by gender and by organisation

Sector in which the organisations were based	Male managers interviewed	Female managers interviewed	Total managers interviewed
SMEs Nine SMEs (smallest 40, largest 280 employees, in various sectors: manufacturing, professional services, marketing)	6	7	13
Health NHS trust (Midlands)	2	5	8[a]
Local authorities Kent Yorkshire Social services department (Midlands)	14	7	22[a]
Financial services/banks Cellbank in Yorkshire and Kent E Bank (Scotland) North Bank (Scotland) Castle Funds (Scotland) Edinburgh Life (Scotland)	18	21	39
Retail – supermarkets Shopwell stores in Kent and Yorkshire	4	5	9
Total line managers interviewed	44	45	91[a]

Note: [a] Sex of one of the line managers in this group was not recorded – two in total.

Table 1.2: Line managers' caring responsibilities when interviewed

Sector of employment (number of managers interviewed)	For children only	For older people only	For non-elderly adults only	Childcare and adult care combined	No current caring role	Caring role(s) unknown
SMEs (13)	9	1	0	1	2	0
Health (8)	0	2	1	0	5	0
Local authorities (22)	6	1	3	0	8	4
Financial services (39)	22	1	0	0	15	1
Supermarkets (9)	2	2	0	0	4	1
All (91)	39	7	4	1	34	6

At least half of the managers had been with their current employer for 11 years or more, and 16 of the 91 had over 20 years' service. The local authority and NHS managers had the longest years' service. Twenty-two of the 30 managers from this type of employment had worked for the same employer for 11 years or more, and only two had less than five years' service. In the SMEs, most managers had between five and 10 years' service. Among the financial services managers with less than five years' service, 10 were based in E Bank, which was a recently formed organisation.

Correspondingly, some managers had comparatively long experience in their current managerial role, while others were relative newcomers in their particular job. Of the 53 for whom data are available, 39 had been in their current post for five years or less, and 14 for six years or more.

Table 1.3 shows the size of the staff groups the line managers were responsible for, by sector. Here we see that the majority of the managers were responsible for a staff group of between five and 49 staff. It should be noted that some of the managers with very large groups of staff distinguished between their 'direct reports' (usually 6-10 more junior managers whom they managed on a daily basis) and the larger organisational unit for which they were responsible. In practice, many staff in these large groups would have first contact with an intermediate manager for day-to-day issues.

The organisations

With the exception of some of the SMEs which had predominantly male workforces, the managers interviewed in these studies mostly worked in large organisations where a majority of employees were female, and where part-time

Table 1.3: Number of staff managed, by sector of employment

Sector of employment (number of managers interviewed)	Fewer than 5	5-19 staff	20-49 staff	50+ staff	Unknown number of staff	All
SMEs (13)	4	3	4	1	1	13
Health (8)	1	5	1	1	0	8
Local authorities (22)	2	6	7	3	4	22
Financial services (39)	2	12	16	6	3	39
Supermarkets (9)	2	3	0	3	1	9
All sectors (91)	11	29	28	14	9	91

working was common, or in some cases, such as the supermarkets, the dominant employment pattern (Table 1.4). These factors mean that most of the managers considered in this report were very familiar with dealing with employees who combined their employment with some form of domestic or caring responsibility. Maternity leave, part-time working and flexitime were strongly embedded within many of these organisations, and the fact that many employees were also mothers had become taken for granted.

Thus maternity leave was treated as a fact of life, and part-time working was recognised as the main way in which many women managed childcare alongside employment. In most of the organisations it was readily acknowledged that some part-time staff, and some full-time staff, also arranged alternative childcare, using childminders, day nurseries, and especially relatives, to provide appropriate support. That these arrangements could occasionally break down, and that children could require short-term care during acute childhood illnesses or following accidents, was widely understood and accepted. There was less evidence, as we shall see, that managers (or their human resources departments) took seriously their employees' roles in caring for adult dependants, or recognised that many of the pressures of combining employment and care could be very real yet well hidden.

The main family-friendly policy provisions in place in each organisation when the research was

Table 1.4: The organisations in which the managers worked

Sector	Organisations in which managers were interviewed		
SMEs	Nine SMEs		
	Technical Services	(1)	*280 employees, 25% female*
	Magnetics	(1)	*98 employees, 68% female*
	The Paper Company	(1)	*50-80 employees, 50% female*
	Diagnostics	(2)	*40 employees, 30% female*
	Electrical	(1)	*260 employees, 30% female*
	Big Agents Surveying	(1)	*85 employees, 35% female*
	The Partnership	(2)	*44 employees, <10% female*
	Chartered Surveyors	(1)	*200 employees, 50% female*
	Woodcare Advice	(3)	*60 employees, 33% female*
Health	One NHS trust in the Midlands (4,000 employees)		
	Unionised, 80% female workforce, 59% of staff work part-time		
Local authorities	One Kent local authority (500 employees)		
	One department in a Yorkshire local authority (18,000 employees)		
	One social services department in the Midlands (5,000 employees)		
	All unionised, majority of staff female		
Financial services	Edinburgh Life (Scotland) (assurance company, 12,000 employees worldwide)		
	57% female workforce, 11% part-time, staff association		
	E Bank (Scotland) (retail and tele-bank established less than four years, 1,000 employees)		
	58% female, approximately 6% part-time, staff association		
	North Bank (Scotland) (retail bank, 37,000 UK employees)		
	82% female, 38% part-time, unionised		
	Castle Funds (Scotland) (investment managers, 200 employees)		
	47% female, 5% part-time, not unionised		
	Cellbank (Yorkshire and Kent) (retail banking, over 5,000 employees in UK)		
	Unionised		
Supermarkets	Shopwell (two stores within the same major grocery retailer, one in Kent, one in Yorkshire. Approximately 400 employees in each store)		
	mostly female part-time staff; not unionised, staff representative system		

carried out, in addition to those required by law, are indicated in Table 1.5. As this is a very rapidly changing picture, in terms of both statutory and voluntary provision, it is important to note that some of the data for this study was collected before recent changes to the law affecting paternity and maternity leave, emergency carers' leave and parental leave[1].

As can be seen in Table 1.5, most of the larger organisations had a wide range of policies designed to support employees in combining work and family responsibilities in a flexible manner. By contrast, the SMEs had not established formal family-friendly policies, but had developed a range of informal arrangements to support employees with family and caring responsibilities. Although some organisations had introduced different forms of *paid* leave, many of the available options were *unpaid*, thus imposing a real cost on employees who took them up, in terms of lost earnings. Some policy options were available only to employees with a specified minimum length of service, or with favourable annual appraisal or similar evaluations of their performance. Many options were discretionary, allowing immediate line managers to judge the appropriate response having assessed the situation the employee had brought to them. The discretionary policies were usually framed within maximum limits, and written or verbal guidance was often available from the human resources department (except in the SMEs which had no such organisational function) and/or in an official handbook or manual.

The nature of the work undertaken in the 19 different organisations, and the labour market conditions in which it was carried out can be described in general terms (see below), although detailed commentary on this is beyond the scope of this report, and available in the original study reports.

Small and medium-sized enterprises

The SMEs were all located in East Anglia, mostly in local labour markets experiencing low

unemployment and significant competition for skilled and qualified labour. Some were delivering services directly to clients, and stressed the importance of nurturing high standards in these relationships. This tended to make these organisations 'time-greedy' and dependent on flexible performance by employees, who were expected to be willing to work outside their normal hours when necessary to meet client deadlines. Senior staff in the SMEs stressed that in comparatively small, private sector firms unscheduled employee absences could be difficult to manage. In some, senior managers believed that certain policies, such as part-time working or flexitime, could never operate successfully – although others offered evidence that disputed this belief.

Health

The NHS trust was a large public sector organisation in which delivering 24-hour services and complying with statutory requirements and national policy guidelines played a central role. Current agendas within the organisation included modernising service delivery, achieving efficiency gains and service improvements for patients/ customers, and adopting workforce policies designed to enhance recruitment and retention and to recognise diversity. In this sector there were also long-standing challenges relating to adequate staffing levels and staff stress. While the Midlands location of the NHS trust included in the study was not an area of the most acute labour shortage for health professionals, it was recognised within the trust that retaining an expensively trained and highly skilled workforce was of critical importance, and in some localities staff shortages were creating difficulties.

Local authorities

Both the Kent and Yorkshire local authorities had faced sharp financial difficulties during and just before the study took place, and both had done some significant restructuring of their organisation, in part to accommodate this. The local authority workers, especially in Yorkshire, were found to have comparatively long service and to work in a wide variety of roles, deploying an extensive range of skills. This meant that few were carrying out tasks identical to others in their organisation, or, if they were performing similar

---

[1] Relevant legislation includes the 1996 Employment Rights Act, the 1998 Human Rights Act, the 1999 Employment Relations Act (which implemented relevant changes from April 2003). For more information, please refer to the end of this chapter.

Table 1.5: Family-friendly policies in the organisations

Sector	Policies within the organisations (additional to statutory provisions)
SMEs	
Technical Services	Part-time
Magnetics	Adoption leave, paternity and emergency leave, working from home, flexitime. Informal flexibility – reduced hours, term-time working, full-time to part-time hours
The Paper Company	Part-time. Emergency leave
Diagnostics	Paternity leave. Informal flexibility – reduced hours, working from home, term-time working, full-time to part-time hours
Electrical	Part-time (administrative staff only). Emergency leave. Informal flexibility for senior technicians
Big Agents Surveying	Part-time. Emergency leave
The Partnership	Part-time. Emergency leave (not offering terms for maternity/paternity leave, apparently in breach of statutory requirements)
Chartered Surveyors	Part-time. Emergency leave. Working from home (administrative staff only)
Woodcare Advice	Part-time. Emergency leave. Telephone help-line, stress awareness counselling, flexibility as staff retention strategy
Health	
NHS trust	Career Break. Carer's leave (informal). Time off in lieu (selected grades). Compressed weeks. Part-time. Informal flexitime. Job share. Limited informal working at home. Dependant leave (five days paid) for domestic emergencies. Compassionate leave (up to six days). Counselling
Local authorities	
Kent	Part-time. Flexitime. Job share. Term-time working. Additional maternity and paternity leave. Adoption leave. Parental leave. Emergency and carers' leave (unpaid). Study leave. Compassionate leave
Yorkshire	Part-time. Flexitime. Voluntary reduced hours. Job share. Term-time working. Annualised hours. Home/tele-working. Additional maternity and paternity leave. Parental/carers' leave (unpaid). Career break. Compassionate leave. Religious observance leave
Midlands	Work Break Scheme (up to five years). Unpaid leave. Time off in lieu (selected grades). Part-time. Flexitime (except residential staff, day services staff). Job share. Pilot working at home policy. Carers' leave – up to four weeks per year after one year's service. Domestic distress (up to five days). Compassionate leave (3–5 days), counselling

Table 5.1 contd .../

Table 1.5: contd.../

Sector	Policies within the organisations (additional to statutory provisions)
Financial services	
Edinburgh Life	Parental Leave. Emergency leave. Paternity leave. Compassionate leave. Flexitime for lower grade, full-time staff only. Job share. Informal full-time to part-time after maternity leave. Career break after three years' service for selected staff. Term-time working has been piloted
E Bank	Parental leave. Emergency leave. Paternity leave. Compassionate leave. Job share. Informal full-time to part-time after maternity leave. Career break after three years' service for selected staff. Term-time working has been piloted
North Bank	Special leave for dependants and compassionate reasons – adjustment to working day or full day's absence. Paternity leave. Career break. Flexible working policy enables changes to hours and job sharing
Castle Funds	Compassionate leave – covers illness, deaths and emergencies in immediate family– maximum three days per year. Discretionary special leave
Cellbank	Part-time. Job share. Additional maternity leave. Carers' leave (paid) Responsibility break. Emergency leave. Career break. Study leave. Compassionate leave
Supermarkets	
Shopwell	Part-time. Shift Swap. Friends & Family Rota (managers). Job share. Flexi-place working. Additional maternity and paternity leave. Adoption leave. Career break. Unpaid leave (older employees). Study leave. Compassionate Leave. Carers/emergency Leave (unpaid)

work (as, for example, among library assistants), they were operating with very tight staffing levels, which limited flexibility. Local authorities have a long history of offering job share, part-time employment and flexitime systems, and these were so well established that they were effectively institutionalised in these organisations. The Kent local authority was in the process of reviewing its flexitime policy during the study period, and this became a focus of discussion in some of the managerial interviews. This local authority was also operating in a local labour market experiencing low unemployment and significant labour shortages, within reach of London's labour market opportunities. By contrast, the Yorkshire local authority was in an area of recognised socioeconomic disadvantage, with above-average unemployment levels, and comparatively fewer alternative employment opportunities.

The Midlands local authority social services department was operating its services – providing services in the community for those requiring care (children, adults with physical or learning disabilities or mental health problems and older people – and their carers) – from a headquarters in a major Midlands town, but with outlier offices and centres across a large geographical area, including some rural communities. The department had recently been restructured, and this, together with the nature of the work in dealing with vulnerable groups, contributed to a perception of stressful working conditions among its workforce, almost half of whom worked part-time.

Financial services and banks

The high street banks included in the study had all undergone recent major restructuring, involving reductions of full-time staff and closure of some branches. Employees were also conscious of the changing nature of banking tasks, which had become more focused on developing and selling a wider and modernised range of financial products. There was competition for staff in the Scottish labour market setting, putting staff retention and recruitment at a premium. However, this was less true in the Yorkshire and Kent settings.

'E Bank' was a very new company, set up to exploit the new technology available to deliver

financial services at lower cost. As such, it had recruited its entire staff shortly before the fieldwork took place, and was operating new systems using a recently trained workforce in a call centre setting. As it was a subsidiary of 'Edinburgh Life' it had adopted many of the formal policies which had been developed in that organisation. 'Castle Funds' was a much smaller firm of fund managers, and therefore had a higher proportion of professionals working long hours.

Supermarkets

'Shopwell' is a major grocery retailer with stores across the UK. Within each store, the workforce of mostly part-time employees delivers service to customers on a virtually 24/7 basis, experiencing high levels of customer demand in the evenings and weekends, and often taking deliveries and stocking the stores outside 'normal' office hours. Over 90% of staff are on basic grades and paid the same or very similar hourly rates. Although all staff receive company training, the levels of skill and qualification required are low, and most employees can be substituted for each other, on the tills, stacking shelves, and in store-keeping duties. This provides an excellent opportunity for low-cost forms of flexibility in managing staff – including the shift swap arrangements which were greatly favoured by staff and which they could arrange themselves with minimal managerial involvement. There was greater competition for this type of labour in Kent than in Yorkshire, but the company's flexible use of students, older (pre-retired) workers, and part-time labour to cover its peaks and troughs in demand reduced the pressure on staff recruitment in both locations.

As we shall see, issues of recruitment, retention, employee substitutability and flexibility, and the stress experienced by staff in combining work roles with family responsibilities arose in many of the interviews. Before exploring that aspect of the data we turn now to a brief note on the methods used in the secondary analysis of the data, and, in Chapter 2, briefly review the literature relevant to the organisational management of family-friendly policies.

The methodology

As already noted, this study relies on secondary analysis of four data sets – the Cambridge, Keele, Napier and Sheffield Hallam/City studies conducted within the Joseph Rowntree Foundation 'Work and Family Life' programme. The methods used to collect the original research data for the four studies are described elsewhere. Here, for the present study, it is appropriate only to outline the approach used in conducting the secondary analysis of selected data from those studies, relating specifically to line managers.

Having agreed to undertake collaborative secondary analysis, the research teams met to discuss the project and agreed to appoint a member of each research team to identify the relevant material for the study. This resulted in pooling of:

- the topic guides used for the interviews with managers in each study;
- details of the methodology used in each study;
- information about the family-friendly policies in place in the organisations studied.

In addition, each team completed a 'line manager grid' (designed specifically for the secondary analysis, giving details of each manager interviewed), and extracted all relevant quotations from each of the line manager interviews, using the list of topics given in Appendix B. This work was completed in the summer and autumn of 2002.

The material supplied by each team was then brought together and subjected to secondary analysis by Sue Yeandle. This involved mapping the personal information and organisational details to gain a view of the whole data set of 91 interviewees, and organising the quotations so that the sex and caring/family experience of each line manager, as well as their organisational setting, could be identified and compared. The data were then searched for themes, which were aligned with the lists of concepts developed in the original studies by the four research teams.

At a further meeting of the authors it was agreed that the report should include a concise summary of relevant literature (Chapter 2), with the main body of the report focusing on the main themes, which had emerged from the analysis. Chapters 3 to 6 thus include discussion of:

- line managers' knowledge of family-friendly policies;
- their attitudes to employees with caring responsibilities;
- the relationship between individual and organisational approaches to policy implementation;
- the concept of 'flexibility' in the management of workplaces and of workers; and
- a consideration of how far organisations benefit from adopting family-friendly policies and approaches.

In Chapter 7, the report concludes with a discussion and a set of policy recommendations, aimed at organisations, policy makers, human resources departments, and line managers themselves.

Note

The *1996 Employment Rights Act* included the right to maternity leave, to paid time off for antenatal care, time off to care for dependants and the right to claim automatic unfair dismissal for a reason related to pregnancy, childbirth, maternity or parental leave or time off for care of dependants.

Arguably, under the *1998 Human Rights Act*, excessively long or anti-social hours may be deemed to deprive a worker of their right to family life. If men and women are treated differently this may also be discrimination under Article 14 of the European Convention on Human Rights.

The *1999 Employment Relations Act* was in part a response to the EU Parental Leave Directive (96/34), which provides both for parents of children up to a specified age to be given unpaid parental leave, and for unpaid dependant care leave.

From April 2003, employees have had the right to request flexible working under the amended *1996 Employment Rights Act*. The regulations relevant to this new right are the 2002 Flexible Working (Eligibility, Complaints and Remedies) Regulations and the 2002 Flexible Working (Procedural Requirements) Regulations.

2

Line managers and the management of work–life balance

This chapter outlines some of the key themes identified in the literature on family-friendly employment policies and the achievement of work–life balance, as they relate to the experience, situation and attitudes of line managers, and some general managers of small businesses, working in organisations where they have responsibility for the day-to-day management of a group of staff.

It draws on the evidence from the research reports of four original studies in the Joseph Rowntree Foundation's 'Work and Family Life' programme carried out by the present authors and their colleagues (see Appendix A), as well as on the wider research-based literature on work–life issues and family-friendly employment.

Background

In the past 20 years, the emergence of the concepts of 'family-friendly employment' and of 'work–life balance' has brought these issues out from their origins in a mainly sociological and feminist literature into the purview of public policy, human resource management and occupational health and well-being. A role for government, in providing the frameworks of equality and sex discrimination legislation, in establishing employment rights and entitlements, and in building an infrastructure of support for what – in the heyday of industrial capitalism – was mostly women's unpaid work (childcare, the care of adult dependants) has finally been recognised and has gained wide public support (Hogarth et al, 2000).

Debates about how people in employment who also have responsibilities for the care of children, for adult dependants or for domestic

management can combine employment with family life have been aired now for well over half a century. The literature in which these themes have been discussed includes: within sociology, a long-standing focus on the relationship between employment and family life; an equal opportunities literature concerned with the achievement of gender equity; and a management literature which highlights the organisational behaviour and roles of managers within workplaces, in which issues of organisational culture and human resources management tend to come to the fore.

Thus the literature ranges from Myrdal and Klein's 1950s focus on *Women's two roles* (1957), through exploration of the lives, life worlds and pressures on 'working mothers' (Sharpe, 1984; Yeandle, 1984; Brannen and Moss, 1991), to contemporary concerns with equity in careers and job rewards (Women and Equality Unit, 2002) and with the effective organisational use of human resources (Kingsmill, 2001). For most of this time, the focus has been on (i) women as individual employees and as wives and mothers; (ii) on the way family life might be affected when women pursue careers or work long hours; and (iii) on women as organisers and managers of their demanding burdens of paid and unpaid work.

Since the 1990s, trades unions have played an increasing role in promoting these policies for their members, culminating in the preparation of *Changing times*, a guide "for union representatives and managers who wish to work in partnership to develop and implement strategies for work–life balance which enhance productivity, efficiency and service delivery – and improve job security and satisfaction" (TUC, 2001, p 3). Many individual trades unions began running campaigns on this theme in the late 1990s, and continue to pursue this aspect of their agenda for their members (Mann and Anstee, 1989; Bond et al, 2002).

Organisations and businesses – particularly those with highly feminised workforces – have taken action in response to social, economic and technological change, as well as to demographic pressures and in some cases to the bargaining strategies of unions. Many now employ their increasingly diverse workers on a wider range of more flexible contracts, deploy their workforces in more varied ways to meet changing business needs, and have introduced a range of organisational policies, including special leaves and other benefits, to address their concerns about the costs of recruiting staff, upholding employee commitment and retaining trained workers.

The development of organisational policies intended to suit employees with family responsibilities, or to enable workers to achieve a balance between work and other aspects of their lives – family, leisure, citizenship, education – has been driven by a belief in a three-fold rationale. This holds that there is a valid 'business case' for the costs of developing these policies, that 'gender equity' can be enhanced through such policy developments, and that greater employee commitment can be achieved through meeting individuals' differing 'needs' through diversity management (Dex and Scheibl, 2000, p 29). It has also been pointed out that technological developments, particularly in information and communication technology, have increased the opportunity for some types of work–life balance policy, even if these sometimes "extend the reach of the company into the home in unhelpful ways" (Evan, 2000, p 33).

A key finding of previous research on family-friendly organisational policies has been that their existence offers no panacea. Some have argued that individual policy options – such as access to special leave – have little impact if offered in isolation, and that it is only "a comprehensive bundle of family-friendly practices" which really makes a difference to corporate performance and the business case (Guest, 2002, p 270, citing Perry-Smith and Blum, 2000). There is also debate within the literature about the relative importance of 'top-down' commitment, of an organisational culture which

values work–life harmony and balance, and of the acceptance by employers and employees of 'joint responsibility' for achieving work–life balance (DfEE, 2000; Hogarth et al, 2000).

Fletcher and Rapoport (1996) see the introduction of 'family-friendly policies' as a 'benefits approach', which tackles only the symptoms of "the complex work–life issues facing society today" (p 143), leaves untouched the underlying causes of tension in individuals' lives, and promotes merely individual solutions to deep-seated social problems which require a systemic response (p 144). Rapoport et al (2001) argue for a different approach to address these problems that they call work–family integration. Accounts of action research in large US corporations provide striking examples of studies which asked questions about the daily interpretation and implementation of policy in the work–life balance field, and which theorised a key role for organisational culture and values, and for beliefs and attitudes, in determining how any specific set of family-friendly policies will play out in practice in a real organisational situation (Lewis and Lewis, 1996).

The four studies that provided the empirical data explored in the present report all drew attention to the central role of line managers in implementing and interpreting policy. These studies highlighted line managers' lack of training in work–life or family-friendly policy, and the tensions for managers between responding to the uniqueness of individuals' circumstances and maintaining equity and fairness across a team, department or whole organisation. In organisations providing a service to customers or the public, managers were concerned about a conflict between adopting a people-oriented approach to their staff and achieving a high-quality customer-focus in their service delivery. The report prepared by Dex and Scheibl (2002, p 28) includes the following table (Table 2.1), based on an analysis of earlier research, summarising the barriers perceived by managers and organisations to the implementation of flexible working practices.

All of the four studies from which the data for this report are drawn included managerial interviews. Each has already reported on the perspectives and behaviour described by these managers as well as on other dimensions of the research carried out. Before introducing the new

Table 2.1: Summary of barriers to flexibility

Factors internal to organisation
- Costs of replacements for career break places
- Family-friendly policies perceived as an 'efficiency wage', not an employee's 'right'
- Dominance of 'linear career' or male model of work
- Linkage made between time, productivity and commitment in corporate culture
- Perception among managers that family-friendly policies will cause disruption
- Management styles based on control and dependence
- Size of organisation

Factors external to organisation
- Tightness of labour market conditions
- Ongoing process of competition and change in the business environment
- Working time regimes specific to the industry and production process
- Social policies and legislative framework

Source: Studies which form the background for these lists are referenced in Scheibl and Dex (1998)

comparative analysis of the data from all of these interviews with line managers, which allows comparison of some of the managers' personal characteristics and experiences as well as of their organisational settings (described in Chapter 1), it is necessary to summarise the key issues about managerial practice which have emerged in other literature and in the studies from which the material for this report is drawn.

Managers' attitudes and perceptions

It is clear – from the earlier studies (cited above) which have explored work–life issues from within the organisations in which people with all kinds of care responsibility work – that line managers exert a very strong influence over the way individuals are treated and enabled (or not) to negotiate the work–life balance which suits their employment aspirations and their caring situation.

Managers have often reported feeling unsure about how to respond to the wide range of requests they receive and to the different situations that arise. Employed parents and carers themselves report that different managers treat them in different ways, and that some managers treat different individuals in ways that are perceived to be inequitable. Yeandle et al

(2002) found that while most managers were sympathetic to carers' needs, they tended to have a varied understanding of the policies they were supposed to implement. As a result, policy implementation often occurred on an informal, flexible basis, reflecting reciprocity between managers and employees. Bond et al (2002) also reported managerial concern about the inconsistent practice which can arise when managers are allowed to exercise considerable discretion.

It has often been asserted that managers with personal experience of bringing up children or of caring have a better understanding, and respond more sympathetically to employees' requests. This has sometimes led to a view that women managers, particularly those with children or caring roles, are more willing to respond flexibly than men. There has also been some suggestion in the literature that older, more mature managers have a more sympathetic understanding of work–life issues than younger, single people with less life experience. Frequently these assertions have been based on anecdotal accounts from employees, who by definition can have only limited experience of management attitudes and behaviour, or from line managers' own accounts, where the sample of managers has been very small and unrepresentative.

Other research has suggested that managers may be influenced by a range of 'biases' in their actions and decision making. Barham et al (1993) analysed data from 184 managers in a large Canadian company, and suggested that there were four main types of bias: 'job position', 'type of dependant, 'self-serving' and 'gender'. In 'job position' bias, managers tend to favour, particularly for others with managerial responsibility, arrangements "that reorganise rather than reduce time spent at work" (p 2). The 'type of dependant' bias refers to managers' tendency to react more favourably to flexible arrangements that reduce time at work to meet childcare as opposed to eldercare commitments. The term 'self-serving' bias is applied to the likelihood that managers will "favour arrangements (for themselves) that allow them to reorganize rather than reduce time spent at work". Finally, the 'gender bias' suggests that female managers will be more supportive than male managers of a larger number of flexible working arrangements, and that managers of both sexes will be more supportive of flexible working for women employees than for men.

Although some research has reported that most managers believe that there is a 'business case' for offering family-friendly employment policies (Yeandle et al, 2002), some writers have also argued that managers' responses are affected by their perception that introducing flexible and family-friendly policies increases their workloads (Hogarth et al, 2000). Indeed others report that managers felt

> ... the policies increased the pressure on them ... not all line managers are committed to the scheme and many are concerned about attitudes of co-workers and clients. (Lewis and Taylor, 1996, p 118)

The present report, in drawing together data from a large number of line managers, in a wide range of organisational contexts, at a similar point in time, has the opportunity to examine the relationship between managers' personal attributes, attitudes and experiences, as expressed by them in qualitative interviews, and to link these to the organisational and policy context in which they are operating.

The report therefore responds to some of the questions posed by Lewis and Taylor:

> What is the impact of factors such as gender ideology, the managers' own family structures and the demands made upon them to participate in family work? (1996, p 125)

It examines how far gender, age, and personal experience of parental and caring responsibilities are factors shaping managerial attitudes, approaches and decision making.

Policies and training

Many studies have drawn attention to the range and variety of policies aiming to enhance work–life decision making (or 'balance') and family-friendly employment. As has been pointed out, merely having a good range of such policies in place is not the same as actively promoting family-friendly employment (Dex, 1999). Nevertheless, it is now accepted within government policy that employers have a

"responsibility to help people balance work and other aspects of their lives" (Hogarth et al, 2000), and recent guidance in the UK has emphasised the importance of "achieving tailor-made solutions" which highlight "employer's and employees' joint responsibility" in these matters (DfEE, 2000, p 4).

Clark has suggested that it is useful to categorise policies into those which offer temporal flexibility, those which involve operational flexibility, and those which develop supportive supervision (Clark, 2000, cited in Guest, 2002). Temporal flexibility offers the worker some control over the timing of work activities; operational flexibility gives 'autonomy over the content of work' (p 270), while supportive supervision 'allows for rules to be flexible' when employees need this to accommodate non-work responsibilities (cited in Guest, 2000, p 270).

Some researchers have concluded that certain types of family-friendly policy are more popular not because they are effective, but because they are "easier to implement" (Barham et al, 1993, p 13; Phillips et al, 2002). Dex and Scheibl's research (2002), and the research conducted by Bond et al (2002), shows that in many organisations work–life policies have developed in an incremental and ad hoc way, and that while this may show responsiveness to the needs of some individual employees, it may cause uncertainty and confusion about employee entitlements and the circumstances in which they arise.

As another study expressed it:

> Many of the line managers themselves were uneasy about their discretionary roles and commented that they needed more training and support in making decisions about staff with family commitments. (Lewis and Taylor, 1996, p 120)

Evans (2000) considers that the development of organisational family-friendly policies arises from four main sources. These are, first, a perception that there is a business case for implementing them; second, wider shifts in the way personnel and human resources departments operate, and in the theories, values and beliefs which underpin their operation; third, a societal move towards achieving gender equity; and fourth, the opportunities presented by developments in information and communication technology.

As many researchers have concluded, whether an organisation develops policies, and what steps it takes to support their effective implementation through training, communication strategies and embedding them in organisational systems and processes, frequently depends on the values and commitment of the managing director, employer/owner or senior management team (Hogarth et al, 2000; Dex and Scheibl, 2002).

Organisational context

The question of top-level commitment and influence brings us to the question of the wider organisational context and culture. Lewis and Lewis (1996) stress the importance of the informal culture within organisations, while Evans (2000) argues that the behaviour of firms in relation to work–life issues is conditioned by wider cultural attitudes towards the family.

While it is widely held that the values and beliefs of managers and employees within an organisation play a vital role in determining how seriously work–life and family-friendly issues will be taken, and how effectively they will be implemented, others stress the structural features of the organisational context.

Some of the barriers to implementing flexible working identified by managers themselves (Dex and Scheibl, 2002) relate to the characteristics of jobs and of the organisations within which they are located. Thus an organisation which, for business reasons, operates 24 hours a day seven days a week, will have different opportunities to and reasons for introducing flexible working hours and shifts, compared with one which operates standard 9-5 business hours.

Moreover, for individuals, their job grade and job type may be deemed more or less appropriate for flexible working arrangements according to the level of skill, the scarcity or otherwise of alternative labour, and the responsibility for supervising or managing others. Comparison of policy development and implementation in different types of organisation has shown that it is particularly in firms with large, relatively low-skill workforces, where one worker can comparatively readily be substituted for another,

that certain types of flexible working arrangement can be introduced successfully (Yeandle et al, 2002). However, Dex and Scheibl (2002) found that this level of substitutability was also evident in some SMEs, even though the jobs may not have been easily substitutable initially. Some SMEs had actively tried to create it by getting their employees to train in different work groups, enabling them to substitute for colleagues when the need arose.

Home–work boundaries

Discussion of work–life issues involves conceptualising 'home' (or sometimes 'life') and 'work', and looking at the relationship between them. 'Border theory' (Clark, 2000, cited in Guest, 2002) suggests that individual workers are 'daily border-crossers', as they move between home and work. This approach fits with the common mid-20th century assumption that effective workers (particularly men, for whom work was assumed to be their 'central life interest') needed to be able to *separate* home and work. By contrast, the European Union has strongly pressed, as a means of promoting equality of opportunity for women and men, for the *reconciliation* of home and work, going so far as to run programmes on this theme and to include it within the European Employment Strategy and Guidelines. In the UK, there has been a strong policy steer from government towards understanding the issues as one of work–life *balance*, sometimes also conceptualised as a matter of *juggling* work and life (Phillips et al, 2002). More radical proposals discuss the importance of work–family *integration* (Fletcher and Rapoport, 1996; Rapoport et al, 2001). This latter way of conceptualising the issue involves adopting a 'work–family lens'. As the authors explain:

> Using a work–family lens to surface assumptions about work practices requires engaging people in a process of reflection on aspects of the work culture and structure that make it difficult ... to integrate work and personal life. (pp 150-1)

Difficulty with work and family integration is usually assumed to be an individual problem, related to a problematic family situation.... By the same token, managers, who are used to seeing these issues as zero-sum, where gains for the family mean productivity loss for the business, may fear they will bear all the risks of innovation. (p 152)

... using work–family as a catalyst for change can result in work practice innovations that enhance both business and employee goals. Indeed, the key finding from this project is that work and family goals need not be adversarial but are potentially synergistic. (Fletcher and Rapoport, 1996, pp 150-4)

Mitigating against this development, and a key issue in at least two studies (Bond et al, 2002; Dex and Scheibl, 2002), was the fact that employee commitment and seriousness about career development was often perceived to be related to the long and additional hours they put in. Hogarth et al (2000) have shown that more than one in ten full-time workers in Britain, mostly managers and professionals, were putting in more than 60 hours work each week. Hojgaard (1998) pointed out that, in Denmark, both work pressure and career structure limit the potential to take advantage of the range of family-supportive policies that workplaces offer.

The importance managers attached to 'work commitment' defined in this way is another feature that is explored in the analysis of the line manager interview data from the four studies in the main body of this report. We turn now to our secondary analysis of line manager interviews in these four studies.

3

Line managers' knowledge and awareness of the policies

In all four studies, the line managers interviewed were asked questions designed to reveal their awareness, knowledge and experience of the family-friendly policies, which all the organisations (except a specially selected group of the SMEs) claimed to have in place. As already indicated, many had low awareness of both statutory and organisation-specific entitlements to flexibility at work. There were a few managers who demonstrated detailed, up-to-date understanding of family-friendly policies, but they were mostly in roles or departments involved in specialised responsibility for the personnel or human resources function within their organisation. Here, we refer to these managers as having a 'progressive' approach. Apart from this group, managers' comments revealed that they could variously be 'vague', 'ignorant' or 'resistant' about the flexible employment policies their employers, or the government, had formally adopted to enhance employee work–life balance. These differences in the way managers understood the policies are discussed in this section of the report, using their own words as far as possible.

Managers with a 'progressive' approach to work–life issues

A particular feature of the 'progressive' managers' responses was that they tended to express the view that employers and organisations have a responsibility to show concern for, and to make arrangements to support, their staff in relation to commitments outside work. These managers spoke of an organisational obligation to improve policies in this field, and some referred to them as 'management tools'. Thus:

"It is about the welfare of employees. You need to bear in mind that people have a life outside of work, and that those things will affect them. To get the best out of staff you have to show empathy. The family-friendly policies enable us to do that, use them to accommodate reasonable requests."
(*female* line manager, *financial services*, Scotland, no parental or care responsibilities)

"It's being able to support staff, and having that knowledge and awareness. It's about people acknowledging the fact that 'I know what's going on in your life'." (*male* line manager, *health service*, Midlands, adult care responsibilities)

"It's a key tool for the way we manage people. The main thing is to ensure that there is consistency in the way we deal with people." (*male* line manager, *financial services*, Scotland, parental responsibilities)

Some of these managers were very aware that attitudes to employees' lives outside work had changed significantly over time, such that certain practices were now completely taken for granted.

"I know that about 20 years ago staff didn't get maternity breaks if they worked for this bank, but they do now, obviously."
(*female* line manager, *high street bank*, Sheffield, parental responsibilities)

Some managers were able to define a range of situations to which they would apply organisational family-friendly policy. In some –

but not all – cases they linked this to their own experience:

"Family-friendly policies are policies which facilitate and enable people to balance the sometimes conflicting demands of work and home, the job–life balance bit…. It's about short-term issues that require you to attend to them. It might be a childcare issue, it might be a caring for an elderly relative issue, it might be your house has burnt down. It could be any personal issue, which has suddenly hit you. The idea is, it's the quick, urgent response that you need to sort out, so that you get an immediate solution put into place, but then it enables you to work out a long-term solution." (*male* line manager, *health service*, Midlands, adult care responsibilities)

"Urgent domestic distress, unplanned hospitalisation … if a school rings up and says your child has been taken to hospital, they've had an accident in the playground, that's easy, that's (time off) with pay." (*male* line manager, *social services*, Midlands, no parental/caring responsibilities)

For some in this group, a progressive approach was also about recognising that employees' orientations to work could be very instrumental, driven by a need to earn wages and fit in with caring responsibilities, rather than by commitment to the organisation or to developing a career.

"We do try and accommodate staff as much as we can for their needs. Obviously we appreciate there is a life out of here. We've got lots of mums who just want to work while the children are at school, on the checkouts, so we just try and work around it as best we can." (*female* line manager, *supermarket*, Kent, no parental or care responsibilities)

Managers with a 'vague' understanding of family–friendly policies

Those managers who were 'vague' about policies sometimes nevertheless displayed quite good understanding of the concept of 'work–life balance', and could be quite strongly in favour of the idea that an organisation should be supportive of employees who were managing family and caring responsibilities alongside their jobs. But they knew few details of the policies in place, were unsure who was entitled to access particular policies and had little experience in this area of responsibility. Many stressed that they relied heavily on their organisation's human resources staff, to communicate information or to supply details in an ad hoc way when needed. As the quotations from the interviews given below show, such managers could be male or female, and included individuals with and without caring or parental experience of their own. They were also drawn from across the spectrum of organisations and localities.

"It's in my head, and it's on scraps of paper. It could do with organisation, but it's time. I've been trying to do a full-time job in part-time hours over the last few months and you just don't have time." (*female* line manager, *local authority*, no carer information)

"I can't remember all of them. I can't name them all, but I know what there is available." (*female* line manager, *supermarket*, Kent, no caring responsibilities)

"I don't know that people know as managers what you are allowed to give people. There is general information from Personnel…. We have a policies and procedures handbook, and every so often we will get a list of up-to-date policies…. I feel stupid about the things I realise I don't know, but I think there is a general 'it's there' but we don't really know a lot in detail and how it actually works in practice." (*female* line manager, *social services*, Midlands, no caring responsibilities)

"Policies exist, but not everybody is aware of them. This is partly to do with communication, but also some of these things are of less interest to some people. Communication is difficult in such a big company, and so we tend to use e-mail, but people can easily ignore this." (*male* line manager, *financial services*, Scotland, parental responsibilities)

"Maternity leave – don't ask me the details, I long ago gave up. I leave that to personnel managers to understand the details of it." (*male* line manager, *health service*, Midlands, adult care responsibilities)

"I think the majority of the changes to practice have been established in the last 4 years. I'm only conscious that the last bit we saw on family-friendly policies was about the parental leave … part-time work with pro rata benefits – I'm not aware of anything on this, although it could well be in the personnel folder, you know." (*female* line manager, *social services*, Midlands, caring responsibilities)

Managers who displayed ignorance of family-friendly policies

Other managers were even less well informed. They openly admitted to being ignorant of their organisation's policies, and tended to indicate that they relied completely on staff handbooks, to which they would refer if they felt it necessary.

"I've not really thought about it. If people here have a problem, we look at the manual, but I don't know about legislation." (*female* line manager, *high street bank*, Yorkshire, parental and caring responsibilities)

These managers, who included men and women managers from a wide variety of organisations, and personal/domestic circumstances, felt that work–life issues were essentially 'common sense'. As a group, they often gave indications that they were struggling to cope with their managerial responsibilities. A few were fairly new in their current posts, or had recently joined the

organisation, but this was by no means true of all in this category. Some openly confessed that they had simply not thought about these issues at all.

"I can't think of any policies at all that are considered to be family friendly. I'm struggling. There's certain things, like annual leave – that's usually very structured within the teams. Possibly the carers' leave. Perhaps I'm giving you duff information here." (*male* line manager, *health service*, Midlands, adult care responsibilities)

"I tend not to think of them as policies. If you were to ask me what the policies were I would be struggling. I think it's more common sense." (*male* line manager, *local authority*, Kent, parental responsibilities)

Those managers who had not previously dealt with employees' requests to use family-friendly policies, or who lacked personal experience of using them, showed particularly poor awareness.

"I've never really thought about it because I don't have a family myself." (*female* line manager, *financial services*, Scotland, no parental or care responsibilities)

"I don't know. I presume (we have emergency leave). It depends on the situation. I have not used it since I have been here." (*female* line manager, *SME*, parental responsibilities)

"I don't [know what there is]. Not having really gone into that one at all. I'm conscious of things like flexitime. I don't really know who of my staff have got families other than my direct reports." (*female* line manager, *local authority*, Kent, caring responsibilities)

Managers who were 'resistant' to the family-friendly approach

Finally, a small number of the managers were dismissive of the whole 'family-friendly' approach, and were 'resistant' in their attitude to policies associated with work–life balance. In the case cited below, the manager was himself a father, so his attitude cannot merely be attributed to inexperience of family life.

"I don't want to be cluttered up with having to read all these things. I have sufficient awareness, my staff are not penalised because I don't know about these things." (*male* line manager, *financial services*, Scotland, parental responsibilities)

In SMEs, some managers, in this case a woman with childcare responsibilities of her own, claimed that there was simply no need for policies of this type. Of particular interest here is this manager's gendered perception of why the policies are not needed:

"No, there is no demand, not that I am aware of. It is a predominantly male environment, a traditional male environment, very male, focused on technology. Only four of our 90 employees are female." (*female* line manager, *SME*, East Anglia, parental responsibilities)

Overall, managerial knowledge and awareness was extremely patchy. The few examples of overt resistance to a family-friendly approach, and of well-informed, professional managers with detailed understanding of the policies, were strongly outweighed by those who had limited knowledge and who were often 'muddling through' by arming themselves with information from handbooks, or making ad hoc decisions, for which, as we shall see below, they had not been trained.

Line managers' needs for professional support and training

As reported in all four of the original studies, most managers felt that they had received no training in how to implement family-friendly policies in their organisation. Some openly acknowledged that they were effectively "muddling through", relying on ad hoc access to the written documentation produced by their human resources departments, and on their own 'common sense' and – where they had it – their experience of staff management. As we saw above, it was only a small minority of the managers who were both committed to and really knowledgeable about what organisational

policy was in the context of a family-friendly organisation. Many were vague or ignorant about the policies, and with this in mind it comes as no surprise that their lack of training and support in this field was a key theme in the managerial interviews.

Most of their comments had a common theme, and this message was heard across all the different employment sectors and in virtually every organisation, as shown below in the extract from the interviews. It was of concern just as much to the male managers as to the female managers, and to those who were managers of some long standing, as well as those who were new in their role. Indeed, newer staff sometimes had an advantage over more established employees, as induction programmes for staff were sometimes the only place where the family-friendly approach was discussed.

"There's no refresher programme. We get bulletins, regional workshops. It is the responsibility of you as a manager to keep up to speed." (*male* line manager, *financial services*, Scotland, no caring or parental responsibilities)

"I haven't received any training. I have been trained in carrying out staff appraisals. If someone had a difficulty with caring for someone and working they might raise it in the appraisal, but then I wouldn't really know what to do about it. I mean, people might be upset, and I might need counselling skills. I haven't had any guidance or training to deal with any of that. Training would be useful; otherwise things could turn out a mess." (*male* line manager, *local authority*, Yorkshire, no caring or parental responsibilities)

"I've not received any training; I have received training in management initiatives and counselling, but not on the specific policies. We don't get any briefing from personnel. We just get information about the leave entitlements and policies in circulars." (*female* line manager, *local authority*, Yorkshire, parental and caring responsibilities)

"The organisation is going through a massive change anyway – we've all restructured over this last year. Different people are in post and different policies are emerging. So I would say training is a little bit hit and miss. I think we have a problem within the organisation with [the training]. I think everyone recognises it." (*male* line manager, *local authority*, Kent, parental responsibilities)

"To me, it's not enough just to have a policy, you've got to go out and show people how to use it, how to interpret it as managers." (*female* line manager, *social services*, Midlands, no caring or parental responsibilities)

A few managers, especially those in the supermarkets and in the financial services organisation in Scotland, did report that this situation was changing, or that they felt communication about the policies was of a good standard.

"We all had shift swap explained to us. Every month we communicate with staff. Managers are given a briefing to explain the policies, what they are, how to do it, why the policies have been put in place, etc. They bring the idea to everyone and explain it. We all had an explanation of the summer holidays off – term-time only working. The briefings usually take place before the policy is introduced, but it's not training as such." (*male* line manager, *supermarket*, Yorkshire, no parental or caring responsibilities)

And one line manager, himself based in a human resources department, commented:

"The intention is that the policies are written in a way that doesn't require training." (*male* line manager, *health service*, Midlands, caring responsibilities)

The comments in this chapter suggest that many managers felt caught between their organisation's broad, high-level goals and missions, which often placed valuing and nurturing human resources near the top of the organisation's agenda, and the need to operate within a set or rules and regulations which had been developed by human resources professionals and – in some cases – in consultation with trades unions. Some managers found it difficult, at least on occasion, to deliver on a progressive and flexible human resources agenda, at the same time as being required and expected to achieve product or service delivery targets. The need for training in resolving the tensions here is a key recommendation of this report.

4

Managers' attitudes to employees with caring responsibilities

Managers' comments revealed a range of attitudes to employees who had family responsibilities and to the way these individuals negotiated and handled their domestic circumstances. Some managers displayed very positive attitudes towards employed carers, and expressed a degree of personal pride in finding ways of enabling employees to reach satisfactory solutions to problems of work–life balance. This group included both men and women, and not all had personal experience of managing family life.

Type of caring responsibility

Childcare

Examples from line managers' comments about employees with childcare responsibilities included:

"One man had premature twins, and one of them died. He just indicated when he would be in and when he wouldn't, and we went along with that." (*male* line manager, *financial services*, Scotland, no caring responsibilities)

"The general culture of the company is caring. If one of my male staff's baby is ill, then – off you go." (*male* line manager, *financial services*, Scotland, parental responsibilities)

Care of adults and disabled children

The interview data also included a variety of positive and supportive comments about employees who had caring responsibilities for older people, sick spouses or disabled children:

"If somebody's got to care for an older person, then if we can find a flexible way of working that allows them to be able to build in those caring needs ... or if we can change the way that people work – we're looking at trying to produce some kind of home working arrangement." (*male* line manager, *social services*, Midlands, no caring responsibilities)

"There's no prejudice because of a person's family circumstances, and everybody is quite free to ask for things. For instance, one of my employees has a disabled child, and they are given informal flexibility to deal with that." (*male* line manager, *financial services*, Scotland, parental responsibilities)

"I've certainly had one member of staff who has actually been in three posts because of her caring needs, of her child who's got severe disabilities. I suppose we've broken quite a number of rules, because we've just got her into posts that haven't really been advertised, but I think the guiding principle was that it was important for that individual to remain in work." (*female* line manager, *health service*, Midlands, no caring responsibilities)

One manager summed up her experience and approach to carers in the workplace as follows:

"The majority of carers I've come across are not shirkers. They are very committed to their job. They actually want to do a good job in the home, but also a good job in the workplace as well, because if they've got an ounce of sensitivity, they don't want to be seen to be doing less. In fact, half the time they're actually doing more." (*female* line manager, *social services*, Midlands, adult caring responsibilities)

Negative attitudes towards employed carers were expressed in the interviews much less often. This may have been partly attributable to the research focus, as managers were likely to think it more appropriate to express their more positive sentiments to the interviewers, and may have concealed some negative perceptions. In the interviews, negative remarks often centred on the potential for abuse of the policies in place, or on the risk that less committed employees might take opportunities for flexibility to extremes.

When to grant leave

There was evidence of different managerial interpretations of what policies should cover. For example, some managers indicated that they would give carers' leave or compassionate leave almost 'automatically', while others were much more cautious and liable to question employees' judgements or honesty. In the quotations below, it can be observed that our examples come from line managers in public sector employment, with comments from both men and women, and from some people who themselves had experience of caring or parental responsibilities:

"People occasionally swing the lead. If the caring arrangements for the child break down, or if the child can't go to school because the child is ill, yes, we've great sympathy for people in those circumstances. But that's not urgent domestic distress." (*male* line manager, *social services*, Midlands, no caring responsibilities)

"If your child's ill, then I tend to use the childcare arrangements really (only) if the child's admitted to hospital or something like that. Some people think they're entitled to carers' leave and don't take any responsibility for making fallback arrangements." (*female* line manager, *health service*, Midlands, no caring responsibilities)

"We did have someone whose husband was having major surgery, and they wanted carers' leave. But under the policy we only gave carers' leave for sudden emergencies, so we said, 'No, I'm sorry' – because you've got the opportunity to make other arrangements. You've got opportunity to take holiday or take unpaid leave." (*female* line manager, *health service*, Midlands, adult care responsibilities)

Poor practices

It is also worth noting that a few managers drew attention to what they felt to be poor practice within their organisation, showing lack of consideration towards employed parents and carers. Below is one example of a manager commenting on his perception that other managers could be negative or unsupportive. Evidence about employees' perceptions of their managers' attitudes, from each of the four studies from which the data here are drawn, is reported elsewhere and is not included here, although it is important to note that managerial and employee views sometimes differed quite markedly in this area:

"I know one senior staff nurse applied for compassionate leave. Her son who is handicapped was going in for a series of serious operations, not at a local hospital. The manager told her she should use her annual leave and time off in lieu. And, to me, I thought, 'I don't believe that!' She's worked here a considerable time ... with a previous good service record – she works to a very high standard. And I thought that was unbelievable." (*male* line manager, *health service*, Midlands, adult care responsibilities)

"The problem is that you rely on people [managers] to adopt the company culture, and hope that staff won't be frightened to tell someone if there is a problem. We once had a bullying manager, and staff under him didn't seem to want us to know. He was asked to leave in the end." (*male* line manager, *financial services*, Scotland, parental responsibilities)

Stereotypes

In their comments, managers sometimes revealed stereotypical expectations about their male and female employees, in relation to how they dealt with care responsibilities within the family. In our data, these comments come almost exclusively from the interviews with managers in financial services in Scotland, and were not typical of the rest of the interview material. The lack of complete comparability between the different data sets, and the fact that the studies did not produce data fully representative of all line managers in each organisation, means that we must treat this observation with caution. But it is of interest that such attitudes did not surface in the other settings.

"Men tend to be more flexible than women in when they can go on holiday, because women have a family, and often they want time off when their husbands have their holiday." (*male* line manager, *financial services*, Scotland, parental responsibilities)

"Maternity leave is used, although women seem to approach this differently. One only took the minimum, because she needed the money, whereas others take the maximum available. Bonding with children is critical, and I would want my wife to take time off to do the bonding." (*male* line manager, *financial services*, Scotland, parental responsibilities)

"More women have time off for their kids. The men in my department are either happily married, or don't have any children, so they don't need it." (*female* line manager, *financial services*, Scotland, parental responsibilities)

Gender equity issues

Other managers, in this case both in one company in the financial services sector in Scotland, expressed the view that, where childcare was concerned, the flexibility or leave required by parents should be shared between couples. This, then, was a plea for greater

gender equity, offering an interesting contrast with the more stereotypical view reported above, and one possibly shaped by organisational culture and values in that organisation. This was mostly shaped by the fact that at 'North Bank' senior managers resented bearing the costs of their female-dominated staff's emergency leave. It did not feature in the line manager interviews in other organisations.

"Married couples with children should take joint responsibility. That is, the father should take equal responsibility. At present, women take the prime responsibility. Many employees have children of school age, so children's illness comes up quite a lot. There is an informal, unwritten rule that both parents have responsibility for the child. If there are repeated incidents, it's always the mother bearing the brunt." (*male* line manager, *financial services*, Scotland, no caring or parental responsibilities)

"For a child's illness I think you can reasonably expect the childcare arrangements to be split between the partners. If one partner takes the first day off, and we pay it, and the other takes a paid day off from his/her company, and then if more time is required we would look at them taking holidays, lieu days, or making the time up. You have to look at the other partner, whether male or female, because you can't expect one company to carry all the weight." (*male* line manager, *financial services*, Scotland, parental responsibilities)

In the Scottish investment management firm, one manager commented on the difficulty of achieving a gender equitable approach in implementing family-friendly policies. It is interesting to note the inconsistencies within this statement, which suggests a tension between managerial discretion and regulations, an issue discussed in more detail on pages 31-33 of this report:

Interviewer: "What do you think the attitude would be if a man wanted to take parental leave?"

"It would depend on the manager. If someone wanted to take it, then the company would have to allow it, because they are in the regulations. I think the man who did ask for it would be a brave man. He would take quite a lot of ribbing. We do still have double standards." (*female* line manager, *financial services*, Scotland, parental responsibilities)

By contrast with the above comments, emanating from line managers in private, financial sector jobs, the following remarks come, almost exclusively, from public sector managers in social and health services. They reveal both awareness of a need for policy on flexibility at work to reflect social and demographic change, and quite sophisticated understandings of employees' needs for supportive policies. Again, this is not to say that managers with such views could not be found in other sectors, but rather suggests that the nature of these public services and the associated professional attitudes and ethos within them, may have enabled these views to emerge and develop more readily.

For example, one male social services manager, with no personal experience of caring or parental responsibilities, pointed out that it will be increasingly important for employers to address 'carers' issues' as the population ages. In the health service, a male manager who had been a carer himself stressed that "the principle that we would try and follow is that no individual is the same". Another in a similar situation pointed out,

"It isn't just elderly relatives; it's like the other bits that many people go through in stages of their lives." (*male* line manager, *health service*, Midlands, caring responsibilities)

Some managers genuinely felt that they had witnessed a change in organisational approach, and that managerial practice was now more sensitive to the needs of employees with family responsibilities.

"I think there is flexibility. I mean, the fact we have got the TOIL [time off in lieu] system or flexible hours, you can come in at half 9 and go at half 3 – I think there is flexibility, and I think – that seems to be fairly well accepted now. [Although] I don't know that there's the same understanding that caring for sick old people is not the

same as getting a child to school, which is a regular thing, the same time every morning." (*female* line manager, *social services*, Midlands, no parental or caring responsibilities)

"There's no harm in operating flexibly. Family-friendly practices are relevant for those with caring responsibilities for children and older people. Basically, people need to live as well as work – it is a good thing." (*male* line manager, *SME*, East Anglia, parental responsibilities)

Others had sufficient knowledge to be able to identify continuing weaknesses in the way carers and parents were supported in public policy, and to show sensitivity to stereotypical assumptions about familial relationships and caring needs.

"Childcare provision seems to be concentrated on the primary school children. And it's great that they're starting to do these school holiday clubs and before and after-school clubs – but I think in the early years of high school there is … probably more of a need, because heaven knows what they might think they can get up to." (*female* line manager, *health service*, Midlands, parental responsibilities)

"Some of the staff don't have close relationships with their mother or father, but they have an uncle who is very dear to them." (*female* line manager, *health service*, Midlands, no parental or caring responsibilities)

The range of attitudes displayed by the managers in the study, as discussed above, were influencing factors in the way they implemented the policies – both formal and informal – which existed in their organisations. It is to this that the next chapter now turns.

5

Approaches to implementing family–friendly and work–life balance policies

Given the differences in the line managers' knowledge and awareness of their organisations' family-friendly policies, and their varied attitudes to employed carers, it is not surprising that differences also emerged in their approach to implementing the policies. Managers differed in important ways in terms of their experience and length of service in managerial roles, in whether they had experience of other organisations, and in how far they were able to draw on personal experience of balancing family, caring and employment when responding to workplace situations.

Organisational factors

The organisational setting in which a line manager operates has a very important impact on their approach. The scope and range of the organisation's formal policies, its response to changes in employment law, the agenda set by senior management, and the length of time work–life or family-friendly policies had been in place were all important factors influencing managerial behaviour. In addition, there were key structural and cultural factors shaping the operational environment in which managers were taking their decisions. These included the size of their organisation or workplace, the extent to which the organisation was 'customer/service-focused', how far day-to-day operations and management were driven by the demands and deadlines set by clients, and whether the organisation was operating within standard business hours or on a 24/7 basis.

Equally important was the recruitment, labour supply and skills context. Organisations struggling with staff shortages or difficulty in employing skilled workers offer a context for managerial decision making quite different from that operating in an organisation which is seeking to restructure and downsize its business. Organisations operating with a large, low-skill workforce had options for flexibility in the way they managed and deployed labour which were rarely available to those relying heavily on highly skilled and trained technicians, professionals and managers to deliver their business.

Organisational values also had a clear impact. These values included the extent to which the organisation was managed using a consultative, partnership approach. This might involve consultation with staff, their unions or other representatives. In such cases, employee needs were likely to have been significant in placing work–life issues on the organisational agenda. Alternatively, the agenda could be driven from the top, and here the values and beliefs of senior managers were strongly influential. Some organisations were extremely 'time-greedy', relying regularly or continually on staff working long hours and being prepared to 'go the extra mile' for their employer. This time-greediness could reflect a strong profit motive in a competitive operating environment, but might also reflect organisational commitment to achieving demanding public service targets, as, for example, in the health service, where employees' commitments to an ethos of care were often strong (as noted in Reynolds et al, 2003).

In this chapter we summarise the development of existing, formal policies in those organisations which had them, and briefly review the evidence about the organisational settings in which the managers we interviewed were operating. We then turn to the managers' own approach, as disclosed in their personal interviews. Managers' reflections on the policies they were asked to operate and their practical experience of using the organisational policy framework to guide their day-to-day management of staff are then discussed. Their comments reveal how they used their managerial experience, the extent to which their decision making was guided by knowledge of their staff and a caring attitude towards employees, and by concepts of fairness, consistency, reciprocity and trust. Most managers spoke about their discretionary powers to interpret formal policies, and some referred to business or service-driven limitations on their ability to respond positively to employees' requests.

Managers' involvement in policy development

When asked to describe and reflect on their own role as a line manager, some of our interviewees stressed the significance of whether or not there had been consultation within their organisation about introducing these policy developments. One social services manager based in his organisation's personnel department explained:

"There's been some consultation, limited consultation. We have a departmental personnel officers' group and it would come through that, on the basis of, 'Here is some recommended good practice, here's a policy, we can take it forward'. So, not 'Do you want this?', but 'Here's a policy that we think you want, do you have any views on it?'" (*male* line manager, *social services*, Midlands, no caring responsibilities)

Several health services managers in the Midlands stressed that policy development in their organisation involved significant consultation. For example:

"Another theme that runs through the work we do – and it's a national thing as well – is staff involvement. The need for a policy can crop up in all sorts of different ways. We may spot it, trade unions may say we think there are issues and can we have a policy on this, or managers may say we're hitting difficulties around how we deal with such and such a problem. Somebody up here will do a first draft and we then get

into very detailed discussion with trade union representatives and we shape that policy to a point where we think it's an OK policy. It's circulated round to managers to get their view and as part of our consultation process as well, every member of staff has the opportunity to comment on it. It's a very slow process in some ways but if you want to involve people it's going to be slow. I think the culture of the organisation – but not necessarily every part of the organisation – is that policies are about enabling people to do things rather than preventing or restricting people." (*male* line manager, *health service* personnel department, Midlands, caring responsibilities)

In the financial services sector in Scotland, senior managers in several of the organisations reported that working groups had been set up to consult on certain policy developments, including flexible working practices. In these firms, however, none of the line managers interviewed had been involved in these committees, or felt that they had been consulted by them. In another Scottish financial sector company, policies were so informal, and relied so heavily on managerial discretion (see below) that managers were effectively setting the policy agenda in this field. One effect of this approach was to make managers rather wary of how their decisions might be interpreted. As one manager responsible for staff in an information systems department put it:

"It doesn't always go down well in the company. You have to be careful not to set a precedent." (*female* line manager, *financial services*, Scotland, caring responsibilities unknown)

Individual factors

Managerial experience

A number of the managers interviewed had considerable experience of managerial responsibility and of dealing with employees[2].

---

[2] Data about length of service was not collected from all managers, so it is impossible to give a more precise figure.

Some had been with their current employer for well over 20 years, although it should be noted that E Bank and some of the SMEs were much younger organisations.

One consequence of gaining experience was that managers developed their own personal 'style' in responding to their employees. In the health service, a hospital manager with six years' experience in her current role observed:

> "I suppose you make up your own principles as you go along really, and a lot of it is from experience, thinking I did that and it worked well, but I agreed to that and it perhaps didn't work out as well. I think the kind of message I'd like to get over to staff is that if people have got difficulties then they should come and talk to me." (*female* line manager, *health service*, Midlands, no caring or parental responsibilities)

In a local authority social services department, a senior manager with over 25 years' experience commented on his own experience and on how he passed this on to other staff:

> "I think it's important that we deal with staff openly and honestly and that staff deal with us in the same way. I would never, ever, advise or caution a manager and say, you shouldn't have done it, if what the manager has done has been to enable staff to deal with a situation. I would, and have, told managers I think in that one you should have been more generous." (*male* line manager, *social services*, Midlands, parental and caring responsibilities)

Other managers with long service records were able to reflect on their considerable accumulated experience of line management, and of observing how others in their organisations managed. Those with extensive experience in a single organisation showed the highest levels of confidence in their managerial practice, suggesting that knowledge of their organisation and its systems enables them to 'bend the rules' or 'play the system'. As one head of service in a local authority put it:

> "There are some who like rigid rules because they can't be contested. They say, 'That's what the book says'. My view is that

I'm employed to take risks, to make difficult decisions which might actually go against the principle of the policy but that is in the best interests of the individual and the council." (*male* line manager, *local authority*, Kent, parental responsibility)

In Scotland, an assistant branch manager with 14 years' service commented:

> "It usually works out. I play the system really. I know how to, because I have been with North Bank a long time." (*male* line manager, *financial services*, Scotland, parental responsibilities)

In some cases managers were able to spell out clearly and in some detail what dealing with a request for flexibility or altered working hours would involve:

> "A staff member would submit to me a request to make changes. They would need to give some degree of flexibility, giving an indication of available days. They should give me their ideal scenario, what they could live with, and what they can't do, so I can find the parameters. I don't look at any one request in isolation. I always open it up to other people. I try to make it a complete process, and not just a reaction. That way we get a better business fit." (*male* line manager, *financial services*, Scotland, no parental or caring responsibilities)

After four years in his role as head of department, another Scottish manager explained the range of factors he would take into account. These implicitly include his reservations about the suitability of flexible arrangements for those in managerial roles:

> "I would consider a number of things. Is it temporary or permanent; short-term or long-term; ascertain the effect on work mates; ascertain the timescales; is it urgent or do we have time to plan? What is the effect on the whole – will it set a precedent? Try and understand the need, and if we can do it, I'm happy to do it. It depends on the person's position, if they have responsibility for people, it's much harder to manage people. [I would refuse] if it was unreasonable and would impact on the

business massively, but they would get a fair hearing, and we would look at all the alternatives." (*male* line manager, *financial services*, Scotland, parental responsibilities)

In contrast, most of the managers in E Bank were recently appointed. One who had come into a role where he was currently responsible for a group of 17 staff explained the procedures he operated:

"Recently we had someone moving from five days a week to three days a week. We had a meeting of myself, team leader, and the individual. We tried to find the best solution. Also, we looked at what it would mean for the rest of the team, in terms of workloads and volumes, to see if it could be accommodated, and what could be done. It turned out it could be accommodated without making other changes. HR were not involved, although they were informed." (*male* line manager, *financial services*, Scotland, parental responsibilities)

Managers with limited experience could not draw on such extensive knowledge of their organisation, or on so many examples of situations they had dealt with in the past, but some indicated that they already operated with key principles to which they were committed. Thus a supermarket customer services manager explained his approach:

"Shift swapping is a good way of them fitting caring in and being flexible, and I don't really have much to do with that. If anyone has a big issue because of care I do what I can, but it is still a business and we have to meet demand, but I'll always sit down with them and take time to listen." (*male* line manager, *supermarket*, Yorkshire, parental responsibilities)

In the same workplace, however, the young personnel manager, with just four years' experience and responsibility for a small team of four staff admitted:

"I haven't dealt with many cases, and when I do I just manage it through." (*male* line manager, Yorkshire, *supermarket*, parental responsibilities)

As we emphasise in our conclusions, it was particularly the younger and less experienced managers who were conscious of their needs for support and training in implementing the family-friendly approach.

Managers' knowledge of their staff

Many line managers were strongly of the view that a knowledge and understanding of their employees' personal circumstances and family responsibilities was important for effective staff management. In the Kent local authority, it was put like this:

"My idea is that when you appoint somebody, you appoint the person you want, and you want to hang on to them, develop them, and make use of them to get the best out of them. And you can do that by helping them in their domestic arrangements. Work is a large part of your life. It is a means to an end, but people have a family life as well, and the more you can fit those together, the better you are in terms of an employer." (*male* line manager, *local authority*, Kent, parental responsibilities)

A woman manager in the same organisation shared this view, but revealed that the priority she placed on staff being able to fulfil important familial responsibilities had not always been communicated effectively to staff. This statement picks up a theme frequently noted in the literature on employees, that they may lack confidence in making requests relating to work–life balance, and often feel guilty about them:

"X came to see me yesterday to say that her little boy has been away on a school trip for a week, and he comes back Monday afternoon. We have one slot in the diary which is immovable, which is the Monday afternoon management meeting – and she came in terribly worried and apologetic to ask if she could leave the meeting early. This one this coming Monday is the most crucial one of the year, really, but I felt awful about the fact that she felt guilty asking. She needs to go because she wants to meet him coming back from his school trip, and doesn't want him to lug his suitcase down through town to after-school club. I've been annoyed when they've arranged meetings that have clashed with the Monday afternoon meeting, and we've all agreed that we will never do that, but to have a one-off like that is exceptional." (*female* line manager, *local authority*, Kent, caring responsibilities unknown)

However, the fact that this approach is not universal in local authorities is made apparent by a manager in the Yorkshire local authority. Although he shows quite detailed knowledge of the employee mentioned in this extract, it is clear that he tries to keep his staff's lives outside work at arm's length. Note the explicit link made by this manager between his gender and his attitudes. Interestingly, very few of our other interviewees made such comments.

"One person who has had her days reduced from five to four to look after her children would have started to look for other employment opportunities, so it's helped us to retain her skills. It helps her catch up on things like housework, and so on. But I never really discuss that with her. It's a man thing, I suppose. If I don't ask about the situation, I don't get told about the problems. Perhaps I should be more proactive and talk to staff about these sorts of issues. It's not something us men are good at." (*male* line manager, *local authority*, Yorkshire, no parental or care responsibilities)

Other managers tended to emphasise the sympathy they brought to their relations with employees facing distressing family situations:

"A lady in one of my sections, her mother was terminally ill. I think we just took the compassionate view really, that the priority was to be at home rather than here. Her colleagues rallied round her as well, and we were covering for her. In the end she took about two weeks off and we gave most of that as compassionate leave. It's just prioritising, isn't it?" (*male* line manager, *local authority*, Kent, parental responsibilities)

"I will always know if someone has got illness in the family. I've just had a 'phone call today from one of the health carers – her mum's died, and I was able to put that

in context, to say, oh, it's not that long since her dad died." (*female* line manager, *health service*, Midlands, no parental or caring responsibilities)

But some other managers claimed that empathy and understanding were by no means sufficient qualities in a manager, or within an organisation, to ensure good practice:

"I think when we're confronted with these situations, for example a partner of a member of staff who might have a serious or life-limiting illness, we get lost in sympathy and emotion, rather than having foolproof ways of dealing with that kind of situation." (*male* line manager, *social services*, Midlands, parental responsibilities)

Small organisations may be especially conducive to a sharing of knowledge about the personal circumstances of employees, as the following extract shows. Here we can see the responsiveness and effort made by one line manager in a small business when he encountered an employee who was struggling to balance her personal circumstances and her work. This account also indicates the amount of managerial effort and flexibility that may sometimes be required to accommodate particular situations.

"One of my team members now works part-time. She had a lot of time off sick and I discussed it with her, and her GP said it was ME. We had to come to an agreement, so we sat down and reviewed the situation. We agreed that she would work Monday, Tuesday and Wednesday mornings. What she found was a build-up of headaches. By the end of the week she was hopeless. So we changed it so that she came in the afternoon, so she had the mornings to recover. We put that in place and it worked for six months. She is quite young. Then she became pregnant and continued through that time. Then she lost the baby. Then she was off work for several weeks. Then she came back to work full-time and was fine. Now she is pregnant again. So we will work out a new pattern when things develop." (*male* line manager, *SME*, East Anglia, parental and caring responsibilities)

Fairness, consistency and trust

As well as, in many cases, expressing concern for their staff's well being, managers also took the view that it was their task to be fair and consistent in their dealings with staff. This was not easy, as most were very conscious of the wide range of possible situations which could arise, and that even where the circumstances underlying a request for leave or flexibility were apparently similar, each member of staff's situation was in many ways unique. Our interviewees offered a range of approaches to managing this.

Defining the policy

An initial problem related to how the situation – and the appropriate policy – should be defined. As one put it, expressing a view which was widely shared:

"The nature of the emergency is important – and I've heard them all! If it's genuine, like John yesterday who got a call from the nursery saying his baby was having breathing problems, then he just went straight away, no questions asked.... I keep a record of all these requests and what the emergencies were. If there are more than, say, three in a couple of months, then I would approach them and ask them if they had any problems or issues they needed to sort out. You have to be fair to the rest of the staff, and if I think someone is 'at it' I will refuse. By and large people don't abuse it, but there will always be people who do.... It would be paid, but it would depend on the emergency. If it is to do with family and kids, then they will get paid. In the case of the guy who had to go home because he thought he'd left the iron on, he worked it up." (*male* line manager, *financial services*, Scotland, caring responsibilities unknown)

Yet there was also awareness that things tended to be more complicated than this, although those who were managing established and trusted staff felt able to rely on the integrity of their employees:

"If it is something to do with a child's illness, then there is no question, they have to go. I have found that what one person sees as an emergency another doesn't. [But] all the people here are reasonable and I just don't think they would ask if it wasn't necessary." (*female* line manager, *financial services*, no care responsibilities)

Others were less confident that staff could be relied on to place proper emphasis on their employment responsibilities, however:

"Some staff do think that they can have a lot of leniency with regard to hours, etcetera, because of family-friendly policies, but don't seem to realise that they have to have regard for service delivery." (*male* line manager, *local authority*, Yorkshire, no care responsibilities)

"I manage 25 people. This team is home-based. Most of them have computer link-up facilities for connecting into the company. I do sometimes think, 'Are they working?'.... We do have some issues when they say they are at work [travelling team] and then I find them at home." (*male* line manager, *SME*, East Anglia, caring responsibilities unknown)

"People can take advantage. People can destroy [flexibility] when the company has offered it. But I have not had any problems, nor anywhere else in the company to my knowledge." (*male* line manager, *SME*, East Anglia, parental responsibilities)

Operational flexibility

Those managing more senior employees tended to be the most confident about the way their staff would respond to pressures in their personal and family lives:

"They don't need my permission to take time off because my philosophy is about delegation anyway. All the staff we have are professional staff.... The staff I have run jobs, they know they are responsible, they know the implications of their own decisions, so when they take time off or someone from the group takes time off, the group supports them. People are basically responsible. If you give them responsibility, they respond." (*male* line manager, *local authority*, Kent, parental responsibility)

Some managers expressed the view that family-friendly policies were potentially open to abuse, although few could cite any actual incidents of this.

"[It depends on] how reliable an employee they are, how long they have been here – so then you are sure they are genuine. I don't have any chancers in this department, but they do exist in the big wide world.... I might possibly make it unpaid if the person was new and I was not sure of them, so as not to encourage them to take time off." (*female* line manager, *financial services*, Scotland, parental responsibilities)

Indeed there was a perception that their own teams of staff could be trusted not to abuse any latitude they were given:

"If they say it is an emergency, then I trust them. Even if they have to stay in because it was the only time they could get a plumber in, for example. Anything really. [I would refuse] if it wasn't justified, but it would have to be pretty extreme. We expect people to have more respect than that." (*female* line manager, *financial services*, Scotland, parental responsibilities)

"If it was one of my direct reports, they would never 'phone at the last minute, unless it was an emergency. I trust them. I would take into account the reason, but I've never had an issue." (*female* line manager, *financial services*, Scotland, caring responsibilities)

Reciprocity

Nevertheless, being fair and consistent was also complicated by managerial evaluations of the commitment and effort which an individual member of staff had been giving to the organisation:

"It's not about treating everyone the same. Not everyone gives the same level of commitment, some people will stay on and help you out, and you have to recognise

that." (*female* line manager, *financial services*, Scotland, parental responsibilities)

"You need to find a balance between individual and company needs. I will discuss it with the employee privately. The employee's record could influence the outcome. For example, if someone is regularly late. Also personality and flexibility. If they won't give an inch, neither will I." (*female* line manager, *financial services*, Scotland, parental responsibilities)

Sticking to the rules

Finally, some managers, particularly those with less experience, or who lacked confidence, showed considerable reliance on the rules and regulations contained within the formal statements of the policies they were operating. This was 'playing safe', and a defensive position on which the manager would rely if accused of favouritism or any lack of even-handedness.

"I usually get the policy out, photocopy the appropriate bit for them, and agree whether they can have it or not. It does cause problems when you allow one person to have it, and not another person, because people feel unhappy that they didn't get it, and they didn't see why. And also you have to be careful that you don't encourage people to tell lies." (*female* line manager, *health service*, Midlands, caring responsibilities)

Managerial discretion

Most of our interviewees were very aware that they had, in most cases, considerable latitude in determining precisely how to respond to requests from staff for flexible or changed employment arrangements. Many were also conscious that they were sometimes making a personal judgement about the reasonableness of these requests, or about the genuineness of employees' needs. Some also explained that their responses in individual cases were determined by employee expectation, and by their knowledge that some changes were easier than others to implement. Thus increasing a member of staff's hours, for example when caring responsibilities ended or changed, could be difficult because it had additional budgetary implications, while reducing someone's hours was very hard if there were already serious workload pressures on the work group or team.

The factors managers were attempting to take into account included making a decision about the appropriate policy (discussed above). It also involved determining whether both the situation (how serious? how unexpected? how long-term?) and the individual (established employee or new recruit? highly productive employee or time-server?) merited paid or unpaid leave, flexibility over hours or place of work; an informal response (for example, turning a blind eye to short-term reduced hours, or making a private unrecorded arrangement); or simply trusting the employee to sort out their own solution (usually only considered for professionals).

How managers react to and resolve these questions depended on a wide variety of factors, which included:

- their personal values;
- the constraints imposed on them within their workplace;
- the staffing and product/service delivery pressures currently operating within their organisation;
- notions of equity and reciprocity;
- the existence or otherwise of policy precedents and rulebooks;
- features of the organisational culture, which could sometimes dictate a particular response;
- how confident the manager was about bending or breaking 'official' rules.

This section explores some of the ways managers described the discretion they had and how they felt this discretion was circumscribed.

In the Yorkshire local authority, employees had within recent years been invited, across the board, to reduce their hours as a means for the council to tackle a budget crisis. With this in the background, one manager in this organisation commented.

"Really it's harder to increase hours once they've been reduced, because of the tight budgets. Any decisions are made on the basis of service provision, there is no preferential treatment. I have to make sure that I plan for these things when I do the

rota, and deal with it in an ad hoc way. There aren't any real problems. If I can't allow the flexibility that people want, I do have the discretion to say no, but it's not very easy to do that." (*female* line manager, *local authority*, Yorkshire, parental responsibilities)

One mechanism for operating in a discretionary way was to make an informal arrangement with the employee, usually to cover short-term issues, which would not necessarily be formally recorded. This approach often had the advantage for the employee of their being treated, for pay purposes, as if they had been at work, even though they had not been. A disadvantage, for their organisation and for understanding these practices, is that they frequently remained hidden from all official record-keeping and monitoring of the policies. A male local authority manager in Kent explained his approach:

"If they are putting in their time and giving me of their best, then I will do what I can within the scheme of things to meet their needs and to help those needs."

Interviewer: "And there wouldn't be any wage penalty?"

"Not if I was doing it informally, which is the way I would normally keep it." (*male* line manager, *local authority*, Kent, parental responsibilities)

Many managers spoke positively about the scope they had to treat individual cases on what they saw as their particular merits. Only a few commented, as we know many employees have done[3], on the risk that actual or perceived unfairness and inequities can arise from managers operating in this way.

"I use my own discretion. If people need time off for bereavement issues, as far as I'm concerned that's fine with me.... My view is that they put their hours in, and they work jolly hard, and in time of need they deserve to be supported, however long that takes, really." (*female* line

3   This perception by employees was reported in the original reports of the four studies.

manager, *social services*, Midlands, no parental or caring responsibilities)

"One person's grandparent had died, and in the end the member of staff got seven days off work, it was all paid leave. The member of staff concerned had to look after the other grandparent and make all the arrangements, so I used my discretion to give them as much time as was reasonably required." (*female* line manager, *financial services*, Yorkshire, parental responsibilities)

Others explained the constraints on their discretionary powers:

"I can use my discretion for a half or full day by not registering it, which I am entitled to do – or advising them to use other paid leave." (*male* line manager, *financial services*, Scotland, no parental or care responsibilities)

"I have discretion to make it paid or extend the leave. Most policies are quite clear-cut. It is important to have consistency. Where there is room for management discretion it is clearly stated in the handbook – not that there is much room for manoeuvre, there is a limit to manager's discretion." (*male* line manager, *financial services*, Scotland, parental responsibilities)

Other managers could feel even more limited in their options, and seemed to appreciate the protection from criticism which they felt applying rules and guidelines, rather than discretionary powers, gave them.

"I have to speak to my line manager when making these decisions. It has to be agreed so it is consistent across the bank. The staff handbook is the bible. I would consult it. You can always refer back to the formal policy and state to the staff what the policy is. If they complain that they haven't got what they were entitled to, you can show them in black and white." (*male* line manager, *financial services*, Scotland, parental responsibilities)

Finally, it seemed that some organisations had approval and control procedures which they operated with a very 'light touch', if at all. It was not clear whether this was the way these

organisations treated their most experienced and trusted managers, or whether this approach operated 'across the board'.

"They would come to see me first of all. It needs to be signed off by my manager, but he always agrees to it, it's just rubber stamping it. The control is really here. If there is a squeeze on budgets I would have to juggle the budgets and the holidays. I might refuse in the short term if they wanted to increase their hours, because of budgets." (*male* line manager, *financial services*, Scotland, parental responsibilities)

"Personnel would possibly be involved. We would keep them posted. I would have the final say." (*male* line manager, *financial services*, Scotland, parental responsibilities)

Although some managers liked having discretion and control, and felt it enabled them to manage their staff more appropriately and considerately than might otherwise be the case, others were conscious of the additional responsibility which the discretionary approach placed on them. As they pointed out:

"I think it's more difficult because you've got to remember what you've agreed to in the past. I think it goes back to being fair and being consistent, and being consistent doesn't mean doing the same thing by all people. It's about the principles that you made that decision on, the same for other people." (*female* line manager, *health service*, Midlands, no parental or caring responsibilities)

6

Managing flexibility

Operating flexibility

To many of the managers, family-friendly employment, and policies for work–life balance were almost synonymous with 'flexibility'. The word 'flexibility' occurred again and again in the interview material, and the phrase 'flexible employment practices' was often employed as a generic term for any mode of organising work or a workforce, which did not depend on rigid office-based employment Monday to Friday. In reality, managers' commitments to flexibility at work varied considerably, as we have already seen, and what they interpreted as a flexible approach could also differ, between organisations and between individuals.

To some, the key focus was on the increasingly diverse characteristics of the group of staff employed, and flexibility meant responding to this rather than treating everyone as if they had a continuous supply of unpaid domestic support at home, as married men were once assumed to have. To others, it was work itself that had become far more complex, unpredictable and which now required quick responses and immediate solutions. This meant that older working practices had become outdated, and new ways of working had become not so much an option as a prerequisite for retaining market share or, in the public sector particularly, for being positively evaluated.

It was also recognised that in recent decades, customer requirements had changed quite dramatically. In the retail trade and in banking this was to a large degree about the 24/7 economy, and about managing significant peaks and troughs in demand. In delivering this all organisations, including the SMEs in the East Anglian study, had become more dependent on technology. Technology was recognised as offering options for flexible working, such as working at home. However, some managers were wary of its benefits, fearing, for example, that erosion of the boundaries between home and work might not be good either for the business or for the employee.

In some organisations, flexible modes of working had become embedded and were routinised. This was true of flexitime, and of some informal practices, particularly in those large organisations where most employment was office-based. In others, flexible practices were still quite novel ways of managing work, or were still resisted.

In the first extracts below, managers' comments are positive and convey a sense of pride in the approach the organisation has adopted.

"But we're very flexible in terms of, if people come to us with enough notice, and say, 'I need time off to look after a child, or whatever', then we can grant leave indefinitely. It's not a question of 'We'll terminate your employment' and forget about them. In terms of things like that, I think Shopwell's the best company I've ever worked for. Certainly in caring for their employees, which I think is definitely a good thing." (*male* line manager, *supermarket*, Kent, caring responsibilities unknown)

Managers who emphasised the scope within their flexible approach for meeting the needs employees might have outside of work also showed commitment to this way of operating:

"I think we're fairly flexible in trying to meet people's particular needs. We'll alter working practice to accommodate people where we can." (*female* line manager, *local authority*, Kent, parental responsibilities)

"Flexible working is better than elsewhere; it's very flexible here, especially when people return from maternity leave. I moved from full-time to three days a week after having my first child. A lot of people have moved to shorter hours, job share, etc. They try to accommodate people and then they don't have to change jobs." (*female* line manager, *local authority*, Yorkshire, parental and caring responsibilities)

"The company is 'willing to be flexible' in terms of fitting around people's lives. I went on job share after I came back from maternity leave, and when my job share partner left I went on to part-time. When my son had chickenpox I just 'phoned in and let my boss know I wouldn't be in for a week, it was fine. It is also a culture where you are not expected to be at your desk from 9-5 and are not judged adversely if you go home on time." (*female* line manager, *financial services*, Scotland, parental responsibilities)

In some organisations, managers went so far as to claim flexible employment produced a 'win-win' situation.

"Obviously we have a lot of mothers, especially when they've got young children, you get to the summer holidays and it's, 'What do I do with my children?'. Some say, 'I'm going to be off the whole of the summer'. I will grant them that. Then they might call you and say, 'I'm free so and so. Have you got any hours that I can come in and work?'. I go, 'Great'. It just seems to be very fluid, very flexible. You've got like the core of staff who the department runs round, and then you've got like fringe staff who only work 15, 20 hours a week, who – it's great, you can be flexible with them. It works for us, and it works for them. Everyone's a winner, really." (line manager, *supermarket*, Kent, caring experience unknown)

"It's also about telling people they are adults. If you give people flexibility and ability to make decisions, it's a definite feel-

good factor, and it means the company is less authoritative. Many people genuinely want to contribute to the success of the company." (*male* line manager, *financial services*, Scotland, parental responsibilities)

In a small business, it was also explained as a two-way process, and in this case also as a way of dealing with employee 'guilt' about caring and family needs:

"The company is 'very understanding' of employees' needs and very flexible. Informal flexitime is in operation. Others, and I, might have to go home early. But other times I am here till 8 pm. It is a flexible arrangement; I feel I am putting in more, so I do not feel guilty." (*female* line manager, *SME*, East Anglia, parental responsibilities)

Some managers felt that it was now part of their organisation's culture to value what employees achieved, rather than how long they spent achieving this, or where the work was carried out. This could be expressed in terms of 'inputs and outputs', as in the first case below, or seen as part of a culture of reciprocity between employees and their managers, where an adaptable approach on both sides was likely to yield maximum organisational benefits.

"Managers are often flexible in the council in the way in which people work, and are more output orientated rather than input orientated. There isn't much written guidance which is good, because every case is different and so you have to be flexible." (*male* line manager, *local authority*, Yorkshire, no caring or parental responsibilities)

"I understand where people are coming from because I have kids. I am flexible about when and where people work. People have the technology at home, so they are able to work from home. Unofficially people work very different hours. Because of the nature of the job, we have that flexibility." (*male* line manager, *financial services*, Scotland, parental responsibilities)

Technological support could be an important component of this, although the risk that working from home could turn into overworking, or never being able to switch off from work demands, was understood by some managers.

> "We provide managers with laptops so that they can work at home. Employees can change hours from mornings to evenings. The flexibility is reciprocal – employees will be flexible for the company in return." (*male* line manager, *SME*, East Anglia, parental responsibilities)

To one manager in an SME, a key problem with flexitime was a risk that:

> "… you would end up working longer hours at home because there is no control over the working day." (*male* line manager, *SME*, East Anglia, parental responsibilities)

The managers' comments sometimes revealed that there were continuing disagreements within organisations about whether flexible employment, and a particular form of it, flexitime, was a good thing for the organisation.

> "Flexitime is our main family-friendly policy. I would like to see this organisation be more flexible. We are going through a debate within the organisation at the moment, about trying to restrict the flexibility to avoid people taking two days off at once each month. I agree that we don't want to be in a position where people feel they can take two days off a month routinely, but it shouldn't restrict managers from using common sense and saying, 'Take three or four days off, and when you're ready, come back, and in your own time make up the difference'. I would like to be able to say that. I would hate to be constrained from using that sensible approach." (*male* line manager, *local authority*, Kent, parental responsibilities)

Some of the most serious concerns about flexible employment practices were expressed by staff in SMEs:

> "Our main concern is to keep clients; we cannot allow staff to work on their own agenda. Flexitime would create difficulties because you have to work around clients, and you have to be in the office to meet with them and handle their requests."

(*male* line manager, *SME*, East Anglia, parental responsibilities)

> "I personally would not like to see flexitime introduced. It is easier to handle when people are not clocking up hours. When people have challenges in life you have to be flexible to a degree, but outside of that you need a rigid structure to work with. It comes back to the workload; you have to get the work done." (*male* line manager, *SME*, East Anglia, parental and caring responsibilities)

> "I know that flexitime is supposed to be for the company's benefit, but it would not work here. There are not enough people to cover the early and late periods. There is a general preference in the company that people do not work part-time or flexitime. If it was applied in our department I think the company would be at a disadvantage. It would not be practical. The company relies on people working a bit extra to get the work done. Most people have a very responsible attitude to work." (*female* line manager, *SME*, East Anglia, caring responsibilities)

However, the interview extract below suggests that some senior managers in SMEs took a rather different view:

> "Head office sent out a formal memo to all managers to raise awareness of flexibility and how to employ the right person and to take care not to lose them." (*female* line manager, *SME*, East Anglia, parental responsibilities)

> "I've got a lady who's a student and she works in a museum, a part-time job, and she works more hours in the holidays than she does in term-time to fit in around her college course. It's a flexible arrangement between her and the line manager, but in general we don't offer term-time jobs. We don't find we have the peaks and troughs in the business in the council offices." (*male* line manager, *local authority*, Kent, parental responsibilities)

Even in large organisations, managers could feel that the benefits of flexible employment depended on how opportunities were negotiated, and on the attitude of the worker concerned:

"It depends on the type of job they do. It also depends on the member of staff, if they are willing to fit in with workload flow. For instance, I had someone who wanted to work contracted hours and have an extra day off. I couldn't have done this if they'd wanted a Monday or Friday, because these are two of the busiest days, but she wanted a Wednesday, so that was fine." (*male* line manager, *financial services*, Scotland, no caring or parental responsibilities)

It was understood that firms operating in localities where labour was comparatively scarce, or whose business required highly skilled personnel who might be difficult to recruit, might find flexibility necessary as a way of attracting staff:

"If you can get loads of staff, you don't need to be flexible." (*male* line manager, *health service*, Midlands, caring responsibilities)

Others, aware of the costs of recruitment even for routine jobs, felt the approach had more universal benefits:

"One person said she was going to leave because she didn't have a childminder. I changed her shifts, and she has stayed, so she's benefited because she would have been out of work otherwise." (*male* line manager, *supermarket*, Yorkshire, no parental or caring responsibilities)

However, the informality associated with flexible employment in some managers' minds sat poorly with a formal system of flexitime, which could tie all parties into quite a rigid system:

"Most people can go part-time if they want. The exception is my secretary who has to be here for a certain number of hours, but even she doesn't work a regular pattern. As long as I know when she is going to be in, I'm happy. I don't monitor attendance. To work here you should be able to cope with the flexibility and want it. Some bits of work will be tough, and they will have to work extra hours, which they are able to

take back. I let people change their hours. Being informally flexible for people who are on the flexitime system can be tricky, because they clock in and out and have to calculate that within the normal working hours – I did ask if they wanted to come off the flexitime system, but people wanted to keep it. They like knowing exactly how much time is owed to them." (*male* line manager, *financial services*, Scotland, parental responsibilities)

Other organisations were trying to manage flexibility by introducing systems to support it, which did not make hard and fast commitments to their employees, but indicated that they were willing to help them if circumstances permitted.

"We keep a list of people who want to change their hours, and so try and accommodate that change by changing other people's hours. For example, one person might want to reduce hours, and another increase them, and then we can cater for that quite easily. Usually, though, the decision in these cases depends on the branch. If it is a quiet branch we may not be able to increase hours, and if it's a busy branch, we may not be able to reduce hours. But the people can always swap branches." (*female* line manager, *high street bank*, Yorkshire, parental responsibilities)

Do managers believe their organisations benefit from flexible practices?

This report can only explore whether family-friendly policies benefit organisations through the perceptions of managers, as the available data, and indeed the original design of the four studies, do not include detailed information on the costs to organisations of those situations which the family-friendly approach seeks to avoid. These include unauthorised absence; the resignation of staff whose work and family circumstances are no longer compatible; and the consequent costs of recruiting, perhaps from a limited pool of only those applicants who can cope with rigid and standardised employment practices. In all the four studies on which this report draws, it was noted that most organisations were poor at monitoring and recording the up-take of family-friendly and other flexible employment policies.

Some of the organisations included in the studies discussed here had introduced their family-friendly policies in the belief that there was a hard economic business case for doing so. Many of their managers, operating within this policy framework, had reached the same conclusions. Their evidence was cumulative and subjective, but the view they expressed often seemed to be considered and sincerely held, contributing in some cases to a willingness to trust their employees, and to adopt a management style which encouraged employees to be open about their family and caring commitments.

Recruitment and retention

The strongest theme was that having flexible employment policies aided staff retention and enabled firms to recruit the best staff. Here there was quite strong endorsement of the senior management rationale that underpinned the original adoption of the policies, and commitment to organisational goals. Aspects of this included building the organisation's image and reputation within the locality, as in these examples.

"In this city it is a very competitive environment, and we have to be seen to be a good employer if we are to attract good staff. It is also to show respect to people who are already here. Recruitment and retention is the key." (*male* line manager, *financial services*, Scotland, no caring or parental responsibilities)

"The organisation is seen as a reasonable employer, which is the aim of the council. Secondly, there is no point in staff being at work if they have family issues to deal with, because they won't do their job properly anyway. It enables us to keep staff, we get continuity of service." (*male* line manager, *local authority*, Yorkshire, no caring or parental responsibilities)

"The company wants to be seen as a caring employer, plus the pressures of a competitive marketplace. To reduce staff turnover and to attract new people. You won't give your all if you are worrying about things at home." (*female* line manager, *financial services*, Scotland, parental responsibilities)

Performance issues

In the following examples we see that some managers were not only convinced about the impact on retention and recruitment, but also felt the policies enhanced performance, and were crucial in reaping the rewards of expensive investments in staff training.

"I think it helps to attract quality people. It is the right thing to do. It means I am able to get the best out of people. They know I'll be flexible with them, so it builds a good working relationship, trust. I know they won't come to me with unreasonable requests." (*female* line manager, *financial services*, Scotland, parental responsibilities)

"We have a lot of good workers, and it's not worth losing them. There's the training costs, recruitment costs, etc. It's best to do what you can to keep good workers." (*male* line manager, *supermarket*, Yorkshire, no caring or parental responsibilities)

"The council benefits, simply through the loyalty you get from employees. Staff will work for you if you are fair with them." (*male* line manager, *local authority*, Kent, parental responsibilities)

"It is a forward thinking company that likes to take advantage of the new employment legislation. A happy workforce that feels it has ownership of the business will work harder. There are cost savings that flexible working can deliver. In the medium to long term it can help with the retention of quality staff by tailoring their work side to their domestic side. Treat people with dignity and show them support. It allows employees to have a sense of responsibility to the company. In the short term it improves morale and motivation, in the long term it improves retention." (*male* line manager, *financial services*, Scotland, parental responsibilities)

"There tends to be less labour turnover; less people leaving because they can't get the hours they want."

Interviewer: "Does the company benefit from these policies?"

"Definitely. Turnover would be massive if we didn't ask the questions and do anything about them. It's such a short-term thing, and people are prepared to resign over it because obviously it's important to them. They are fully trained, they know the way the company works, and some of them are staff that we want to keep, so that is in our benefit. Plus, every person we employ in the company costs us £3,500. So it's in our interests to keep the people we've got so we don't have to keep replacing them all the time." (*female* line manager, *supermarket*, Kent, no caring or parental responsibilities)

Health and wellbeing

Other managers commented on improvements in staff health and wellbeing, with consequent better management of sickness costs.

"We have shift swaps now. I use it a lot in my department – and I get a lot less sickness in my department than in the rest of the store." (*female* line manager, *supermarket*, Kent, caring experience unknown)

"I think there's definite advantages, yes. Because they're happy, hopefully, and you're helping them, aren't you, and you might be keeping them at work when otherwise they'd be off with stress or some other sickness, and retaining staff. There may be staff who would have to give up their jobs completely if they couldn't work, you know, either reduced hours, or flexibly, for what might be a short-term reason – or even long-term." (*female* line manager, *health service*, Midlands)

"To attract staff, to meet legislative requirements and because of the staff association. Staff are happier, less pressurised, and feel like there is support there for them." (line manager, *financial services*, Scotland)

Risks and disadvantages

A few managers acknowledged some difficulties as well:

"We lose the skills and experience of people if we don't, and it's worth keeping these people. Also, it helps develop the line manager as a person, when the staff come to us with an issue, it makes us aware of it and we can learn from it. One might be that by accommodating the difficulties of one person, as a spin-off it puts increased pressure on other employees. For example, when I let one of my girls [sic] work a four instead of a five-day week, it increases the workload of others on that fifth day when she's not in." (*male* manager, *local authority*, Yorkshire, no caring or parental responsibilities)

But overwhelmingly the message was that:

"Recruiting and training staff takes time and money and it's crazy to lose good experienced colleagues because of a change in their personal circumstances." (*male* line manager, *financial services*, Scotland, no caring or parental responsibilities)

A few managers mentioned that there was a strong corporate approach supporting family-friendly employment within their organisation. The policies are important:

".. to make an attractive package to recruit and retain good people. Some provisions are to protect the individual, and some are to protect the company. In general the company view is that people are important, and we should treat them fairly across the company." (*male* line manager, *financial services*, Scotland, parental responsibilities)

As indicated earlier, a few of the interviewees mentioned that family-friendly policies also carried risks, although these managers tended to feel the risk of abuse of the policies or breaches of trust were well balanced by advantages, especially when the policies could be operated in

a discretionary manner. They also indicated a
willingness to respond to high-level
organisational leadership on these issues.

"There will always be people who take
advantage. The business could suffer. But
it depends on how many people continue
to give 100%. Any company would fear
losing control. How do you keep tabs on
what people are doing? The supportive
aspect of management is the key. Guiding
people, also helping them to make the right
decisions. Not very many people do work
well on their own at home. So you have to
make judgements based on the individual's
needs and their personality." (*female* line
manager, *SME*, East Anglia, parental
responsibilities)

Notably, very few managers mentioned
improvements in industrial relations within their
organisation, perhaps reflecting the low profile of
trades union activity in this field in the accounts
of those interviewed.

7

Conclusions

Discussion

This report has explored line managers' knowledge and awareness of family-friendly employment in their own organisations. In relation to this aspect of their work, four broad categories of line manager – progressive, vague, ignorant and resistant – have been identified. The majority of the managers included in the four studies had either 'vague' understandings of the policy framework they were expected to be operating, or were ignorant about it. Both male and female managers were found in each of the categories, and having personal experience, either of parenthood or of caring for adult dependants, did not determine which category managers fell into.

Some of the differences between the managers were linked to the nature of the organisations which employed them. The wide range of organisations from which the interview material was drawn was described in Chapters 1 and 2 (and the Appendix), and the significance of the nature of each organisation's business and corporate values or ethos were taken into account. This showed that it was considerably easier, more important and more attractive for some organisations to offer and develop family-friendly policies and strategies to support work–life balance than it was for others.

Individuals also varied in their support for and attitude towards both the policy framework within their organisation, and towards those of their staff who had parental or caring responsibilities. These factors were linked to managers' experience, and to their ability to draw on a bank of informal knowledge about their staff. Generally, managers were sympathetic towards those staff who encountered stress in

their personal lives or who needed to change their working arrangements to fit in with changes in their domestic responsibilities. Only limited evidence of stereotyping was found, and many of the managers were sensitive to the changes in social and family life which were driving the work–life agenda. Few managers felt they needed to address problems about abuse of policies. Although some indicated that they would be concerned if this happened, most felt that abuse of policies was not a significant problem, as they did not have staff who were unreliable or likely to take unfair advantage.

Managers placed a strong emphasis on certain key values in their dealings with staff: most important among these were fairness, consistency and trust. In practice, many operated within a system of reciprocity, offering flexibility and latitude to employees, and expecting commitment and a willingness to 'rise to the occasion' if work demands suddenly increased. Few seemed aware of the tensions generated by this reciprocal approach, which tends to idealise those workers who, at least for some of their career within the organisation, can demonstrate dependability, reliability, hard work, often long hours and flexibility.

Managers liked to have discretion, and many felt they had considerable discretionary authority in deciding about changes in working hours, or how to handle emergency situations. Nevertheless some felt threatened by this, and indicated that they needed more support and guidance in taking their decisions, which could well set precedents or affect future employee expectations.

Flexibility was emphasised as central to the family-friendly agenda. Most managers

41

considered that they were flexible in how they responded to employees, and suggested that this flexibility was good for the organisation. Many were convinced by the 'business case' for operating in a family friendly way, often linking work–life issues to cost reduction and effective management of recruitment, retention and absence.

This analysis of in-depth interviews with 91 line managers offers a new empirical contribution to the literature on the practicalities of implementing family-friendly employment policies. While it cannot claim to be representative of all British line managers, the study offers new insights into the way managers in a range of different types of organisation respond to policy developments in their own places of employment. It also identifies and assesses the attitudes, beliefs, experience and knowledge which they bring to their job of managing the performance and behaviour of their teams of employees, many of whom have demanding and not always predictable responsibilities outside work, for children and for adult dependants.

The study has not evaluated the impact of managers' behaviour on those aspects of organisational practice which can be objectively measured – output, individual performance, recruitment and retention levels and productivity. This was beyond the scope of the present study, which did not have access to organisational data on these matters. The study has, however, been able to provide an assessment of what managers say about their own practice as managers. It has explored their attitudes to their staff, their knowledge of existing policies in their organisations, their views about the usefulness and effectiveness of those policies, and their beliefs about how they personally take the often difficult managerial decisions which confront them in dealing with diverse staff groups.

It is clear from the evidence in this study that managers' approaches to implementing family-friendly policies cannot simply be 'read off' from their own personal characteristics. There is no evidence in this study that being female necessarily makes a manager more aware than her male counterpart of organisational policies promoting family-friendly employment, or more sympathetic, responsive or fair to employees. Neither does a simple analysis of whether or not

a manager has any direct personal experience of parenthood or caring enable us to make such a judgement – although some managers themselves believed that they were drawing on personal experience in taking decisions about flexibility and family-friendly policy implementation.

This is not to say that managers' personal experiences, attitudes and values do not affect the way they regard their employees and respond to them when tensions arise between their family and caring responsibilities and their employment roles. This study has also shown that many managers think knowing their staff, and being caring in their approach to them, are important characteristics in an effective manager. Experience of specific life situations undoubtedly gives managers knowledge on which they can draw in making choices about how to respond to the situations they confront at work. Thus being a parent may make a manager sensitive to the needs of a sick child for parental care, or to the priority which most parents will want to give to their children if accidents or illnesses occur. However, a manager whose experience of fatherhood has been one in which his wife took care of all such domestic situations is less likely than one who has shared parenting, or at times had sole parental responsibility, to expect male employees to require the support of family-friendly policies. Our data included examples of managers using their own experience of dividing parental responsibility with their wives as a reference point in their comments about responding to their employees' requests for reduced hours, maternity/career breaks and parental leave.

Similarly with the care of disabled or adult dependants, it is managers' ability to understand the caring needs the employee is trying to meet which is most important. This understanding is likely to be enhanced by direct personal experience, but may also be developed through working in a caring profession, or through having the ability to listen to others and to reflect on and imagine the difficulties and dilemmas they face. Our sample included some very sympathetic and supportive managers who had no experience of caring for older people, as well as some whose own ability to manage caring alongside work seemed to have made them blind to the challenges which others might face in trying to do this.

So our study concludes that while gender, age, and family/caring situation may be influential factors in enabling a manager to develop sensitivity to employees who are experiencing stress in managing work and family responsibilities, they are not prerequisites for this. Indeed, managers can have such sensitivity without ever having direct personal experience of similar situations. In favour of positive developments here is the fact that most of the managers interviewed expressed some desire to be supportive of employees in times of stress, and favoured the exercise of some discretion and flexibility in dealing with the very varied situations with which they could be confronted.

Less positively, we have found that, in general, managers have very limited knowledge of the family-friendly policies in place in their organisations. In practice this often means that they are dealing with employees' needs with their hands tied behind their backs. We found that managers who had participated in training in how to implement family-friendly policies were a very rare breed. Most commonly, managers were vaguely aware of general organisational developments in this field, and had some, although rather limited, knowledge of employers' statutory responsibilities. Among those with less managerial experience it was particularly common to lack any depth of understanding of the policies, and to need to consult the human resources department or to refer to the organisation's policy handbook in dealings with individual staff. We know from evidence from employees (collected in some of the original studies from which the managerial interviews were drawn) that a formal, rule-bound response from a manager can feel very uncomfortable to an employee facing a domestic crisis, and may be resented for years to come.

Those managers who had the experience and confidence to respond supportively when approached by employees, and to exercise the managerial discretion which most organisations allowed them, ran the risk, over time, of acting in ways which might be perceived as inequitable or unfair. This was a real worry for many managers. In handling this, most drew on notions of reciprocity, or calculated the employee's 'balance sheet', in effect seeking to judge whether a generous response would be appropriate, in light of an assessment of the employee's prior behaviour, commitment and contribution at

work. While this approach was widely favoured by managers (and indeed, from evidence collected in the original studies, approved by many employees), few managers seemed aware that, in effect, they could be penalising those whose work performance was already constrained by family roles. The likelihood that this approach involved being most generous to those who, previously, had been able to 'give their all' to the workplace, in terms of the (often unpaid) hours they put in and the flexibility they could offer was rarely appreciated.

This is a very difficult situation for managers, and a point on which many will disagree. Typically, managers make assessments of employees' work performance without reference to their personal and domestic responsibilities, and many would argue this is a correct approach. Others reject the view that an employee who always leaves on time, to collect children from a nursery, or to give care to an elderly parent, and who has occasional time off for emergency situations, should be less positively evaluated because of this. These judgements become particularly important when employees are being compared with one another, and it is thus in the context of promotions and other forms of career advancement or reward that this issue is especially pertinent.

It is very clear in the managerial evidence collected together here that the type of work being performed, and the kind of organisational setting for that work, is critically important. An observation here is that organisations will need, and will be able effectively to implement, different types and styles of family-friendly employment policies according to the kind of business they are in. More controversially, it may need to be accepted that certain types of policy will work better in some parts of an organisation than in others.

Some low-cost forms of employment flexibility undoubtedly have benefits for both employers and employees. Thus in workplaces with significant numbers of employees doing similar work at almost identical wage rates (as in supermarkets) both the organisation and the employees can derive benefits from low cost forms of employee substitutability. These arrangements allow individual employees to flex their working hours from one day or week to the next by exchanging shifts with any fellow employee who is willing to reciprocate. This saves the employer both unscheduled absences (which may be payable if claimed as sick leave) and staffing crises, and enables employees to manage almost all the reasonably predictable demands of family life. Managers interviewed in the supermarkets were well aware of the financial cost of recruiting new staff, and welcomed such low-maintenance policies, which could be easily communicated to staff and, in effect, managed by them, with minimal managerial input. Such approaches, however, although undoubtedly applicable in many other workplaces, including some types of work in financial services, cannot be operated effectively everywhere.

The most difficult tensions described by managers had arisen in customer-facing operations where, because of scarce skills, lean staffing or small operating units, to substitute one employee for another was extremely difficult. There were also difficulties in businesses which were less well managed, and which suffered from poor product pricing strategies or difficulty in controlling workflow. In retail banking, most high street banks have now become small units, often widely geographically dispersed. In smaller SMEs, organisations may have genuine difficulty in meeting output requirements if there is unscheduled leave or if even one member of staff is working reduced hours. These difficulties are compounded in labour markets where recruiting temporary replacements or additional staff is problematic, although Dex and Scheibl (2002) did find examples of innovative approaches to address such problems, including increased use of flexibility.

Organisations nevertheless need to face up to the apparent paradox that, if family-friendly employment options assist in retaining and motivating staff (as very many of the managers interviewed for this study believe they do), then denying employees access to flexible working options may bring a short-term gain against which a longer-term disbenefit must be assessed. Those few organisations still resisting part-time employment are probably the best case in point here. As some managers acknowledged, part-time staff can give even a small organisation greater flexibility over the means of delivering organisational commitments, because part-timers may be more flexible than full-timers about altering their hours. In particular, it was notable

that managers in SMEs identified in Dex and Scheibl's study as offering an 'holistic' approach to flexible employment recognised that in their organisation, responsive and flexible employment practices were an important stimulus to employee loyalty, productivity and commitment.

Many of the managers in large organisations were convinced of the 'business benefits' of offering family-friendly employment. This was especially true where organisations were big enough to absorb the impact of individual circumstances, and could offer employees opportunities in other departments if necessary.

Organisations with marked peaks and troughs in customer demand for their services fell into two categories – those such as supermarkets which had found flexible employment practices such as part-time and variable hours highly suitable mechanisms for responding to variations in demand, and those – usually organisations delivering their services from small units – which experienced a tension between customer demand and flexibility for staff. In the latter, there was a tendency to prioritise customer demand over staff needs and preferences, and it was here that managers tended to be most negative about offering flexible arrangements to individuals.

Managers who were accustomed to operating shift patterns and delivering work 24/7 rather than 9-5 might have been expected to be the most flexible. This was not always the case. In large organisations, for example the health trust, a history of rather rigid shift patterns was gradually being overcome, with more flexibility being introduced. However, staff shortages, especially among skilled staff, were a barrier to some types of family-friendly employment, and some managers felt torn between their desire to respond supportively to employees' needs and their obligation to ensure that service delivery commitments and targets were met.

Where particular types of family-friendly or flexible employment policies had become institutionalised, some managers found it difficult to establish boundaries between employees' rights and entitlements and their preferences and choices. A case in point was the flexitime system in place in the Kent local authority. This allowed staff to accumulate both credits and deficits in the time they spent at work, and to use additional time accrued as a whole or half day's leave each month. Some managers saw this as a good way of enabling carers and parents to manage minor crises or commitments in their domestic situation. Others felt some staff were manipulating the system to take additional leave, coming in early when there was little work to be done, or no one to supervise them, and taking the accrued hours as time off, irrespective of family commitments. Given managers' differing views about what flexitime systems are for, organisations might like to reflect on how they view this particular option – as an entitlement, or as a discretionary support in achieving work–life balance.

A further important issue concerns the role of local labour market conditions in determining how managers view and experience family-friendly employment. Where it is easier to recruit substitute staff, at whatever level of skill, there is less pressure on managers to use family-friendly employment arrangements as a carrot to attract recruits and to retain established staff. Even in the same business, there can be marked differences in the scope for recruiting labour in different localities. To the extent that organisations adopt family-friendly employment as a response to tight labour market conditions, rather than for other organisational reasons, it can be expected that their commitment to these policies may change as labour market conditions fluctuate. It was notable, however, that many managers reported feeling that offering support to employees with caring or parental responsibilities was 'the right thing to do' rather than merely a business decision. How influential their perspective would be in different local labour market conditions is a matter of speculation.

Family-friendly employment has often been promoted as a means of enabling women to gain a more equal place in the labour market. Some managers shared this view. Others were conscious of the risk that these policies could reinforce stereotypical thinking about gender roles, both at home and at work, and become a trap rather than a support for women. A small number of managers showed some awareness of the need to encourage men to take up family-friendly employment options as well as women, although in the present study, this position was taken most vocally by managers in female-dominated organisations which felt they were covering more than their fair share of the costs of carers' and parental leave. The need for employers and policy makers to keep a watchful eye over the extent to which certain types of family-friendly employment can mitigate against gender equity in the workplace is identified below as a policy recommendation.

Policy recommendations

For managers

- Experienced line managers have a wealth of detailed knowledge of employees' needs for support in combining their domestic and employment roles. This needs to be used in the development of guidance and codes of practice about employees and their circumstances, such that individual needs can be taken into account without intrusion into employees' privacy.
- A culture change is still needed in some workplaces to make it acceptable to have, and to respond to, family responsibilities.
- Managers are often a weak link in organisational communication strategies relating to policy on work–life balance. Where work–life issues are raised as part of a routine and regular role for managers they play an important part in achieving effective communication.
- Managers could pool experience of how they have dealt with difficult cases involving employees who are parents and carers. This could be fed into organisational 'banks' of good practice, using suitably anonymised examples. Organisations with sufficient numbers of line managers might usefully consider initiating ways which would enable them to share experience and practice.
- Managers should keep records of the way they respond to employee requests for family-friendly employment or flexibility at work. These should be fed into human resources departments for proper assessment of the costs and benefits of the policies.

For human resources departments and employers

- Human resources departments need to prioritise the development of imaginative training for line managers in the implementation of family-friendly employment. It is unacceptable that virtually all managers are implementing new and innovative policies and legislation without access to training and appropriate support.
- Human resources departments should assess and evaluate the data provided by managers about the take-up of family-friendly employment, and should report regularly to senior management and trades unions/staff representatives on their findings.
- When organisations are restructuring, down-sizing or otherwise redeploying staff, specific attention should be paid to how the work–life balance of staff will be affected. Care should be taken that managers given new responsibilities at these times have appropriate opportunities to develop relevant skills as well as training.

For trades unions

- Trades union involvement featured very little in the managerial interviews. There is a constructive role for unions to play in sharing good practice across different organisations, bringing ideas from one organisation into another, supporting good communications on these matters, and including the effective implementation of family-friendly employment in their bargaining strategies. Good dialogue with human resources departments on effective ways of implementing family-friendly employment should be a routine goal in collective bargaining.

For government and policy makers

- Policy guidance and new legislative developments need to take account of the different organisational settings and of the different labour markets in which family-friendly employment will be implemented.
- Government – not least in its role as an employer – can take a lead by linking the gender equity and family-friendly agendas, and by promoting more take-up of these options by men. This will benefit those organisations which are currently strongly female-dominated.
- Government guidance should include good practice examples drawn from a wide range of different employment sectors and organisations. Specialist guidance may be needed for SMEs, highlighting effective examples of how small firms can successfully be family-friendly.

References

Barham, L., Gottlieb, B., Kelloway, E. and Barling J. (1993) 'But will my manager understand? Managers' reactions to employees/caregiving responsibilities', Poster presentation, Canadian Ageing Research Network Colloquium, Toronto, Ontario, June.

Bond, S., Hyman, J., Summers, J. and Wise, S. (2002) *Family-friendly working? Putting policy into practice*, Bristol/York: The Policy Press/ Joseph Rowntree Foundation.

Brannen, J. and Moss, P. (1991) *Managing mothers: Dual earner households after maternity leave*, London: Unwin Hyman.

Clark, S.C. (2000) 'Work/family border theory: a new theory of work–life balance', *Human Relations*, vol 53, no 6, pp 747-70.

DfEE (Department for Education and Employment) (2000) *Changing patterns in a changing world: A discussion document*, London: DfEE.

Dex, S. (ed) (1999) *Families and the labour market*, London/York: Family Policy Studies Centre/Joseph Rowntree Foundation.

Dex, S. and Scheibl, F. (2000) *Flexible and family-friendly working in SMEs: Business cases*, Working Paper No 9/2000, Cambridge: Judge Institute of Management Studies.

Dex, S. and Scheibl, F. (2002) *SMEs and flexible working arrangements*, Bristol/York: The Policy Press/Joseph Rowntree Foundation.

Evans, J. (2000) *Firms' contribution to the reconciliation between work and family life: Experience in OECD countries*, Paris: OECD.

Fletcher, J.K. and Rapoport, R. (1996) 'Work– family issues as a catalyst for organizational change', in S. Lewis and J. Lewis (eds) *The work–family challenge: Rethinking employment*, London: Sage Publications.

Guest, D.E. (2002) 'Perspectives on the study of work-life balance', *Social Science Information*, vol 41, no 2, pp 255-79.

Hogarth, T., Hasluck, C. and Gaelle, P. (with M. Winterbotham and D. Vivian) (2000) *Work–life balance 2000: Baseline study of work–life balance practices in Great Britain: Summary report*, Institute for Employment Research/IFF Research.

Hojgaard, L. (1998) 'Workplace culture, family-supportive policies and gender differences', in E. Drew, R. Emerell and E. Mahon (eds) *Women, work and the family in Europe*, London: Routledge.

Kingsmill, D. (2001) *The Kingsmill Review of women's employment and pay*, London: DTI.

Lewis, S. and Lewis, J. (eds) (1996) *The work– family challenge: Rethinking employment*, London: Sage Publications.

Lewis, S. and Taylor, K. (1996) 'Evaluating the impact of family-friendly employer policies: a case study', in S. Lewis and J. Lewis (eds) *The work–family challenge: Rethinking employment*, London: Sage Publications.

Mann, K. and Anstee, J. (1989) *Growing fringes: Hypothesis on the development of occupational welfare*, Todmorden: Armley Publications.

Myrdal, A. and Klein, V. (1957) *Women's two roles*, London and Boston: Routledge and Kegan Paul.

Perry-Smith, J. and Blum, T. (2000) 'Work-family human resource bundles and perceived organizational performance', *Academy of Management Journal*, vol 43, no 6, pp 1107-17.

Phillips, J., Bernard, M. and Chittenden, M. (2002) *Juggling work and care: The experiences of working carers of older adults*, Bristol/York: The Policy Press/Joseph Rowntree Foundation.

Rapoport, R., Bailyn, L., Fletcher, J.K. and Pruitt, B.H. (2001) *Beyond work–family balance: Advancing gender equity and workplace performance*, San Francisco, CA: Jossey-Bass.

Reynolds, T., Callender, C. and Edwards, R. (2003) *Caring and counting: The impact of mothers' employment on family relationships*, Bristol/York: The Policy Press/Joseph Rowntree Foundation.

Sharpe, S. (1984) *Double identity: The lives of working mothers*, Harmondsworth: Penguin.

TUC (Trades Union Congress) (2001) *Changing times: A TUC guide to work–life balance*, London: TUC.

Women and Equality Unit (2002) 'Advancing women in the workplace: Key research findings', http://www.womenandequalityunit.gov.uk/women_work

Yeandle, S. (1984) *Women's working lives: Patterns and strategies*, London: Tavistock Publications.

Yeandle, S., Wigfield, A., Crompton, R. and Dennett, J. (2002) *Employed carers and family-friendly employment policies*, Bristol/York: The Policy Press/Joseph Rowntree Foundation.

Appendix A:
The four studies

The Keele University Study (Phillips et al, 2002)

The Keele study focused specifically on how two public sector organisations were responding to the circumstances of the approximately 1 in 10 of their workforces who were carers of dependant adults (Phillips et al, 2002). This study highlighted the diversity of work–care situations, and observed that family-friendly policies designed to meet the needs of working carers were still evolving and being tested in both the organisations concerned (a hospital trust and a local authority social services department).

Managers in these organisations commented on an absence of robust systems of review and monitoring of uptake, and felt that they lacked adequate training and good practice guidelines to support them in implementing the policies in place.

The authors point out that "flexibility, manager attitudes and discretion were found to be key factors in this study" (p 38), and also emphasise that managers tended to feel they were part of a "balancing act between the needs of the organisation and the needs of carers in the workforce" (p 39). In contrast to carers, managers were typically concerned with 'the bigger picture' – "with organisational checks and balances, with fairness and consistency, and with what the rules state" in terms of policy implementation.

The Keele study found that, in implementing policy, managers tended to rely on their "knowledge of their staff, support from colleagues, and the ability to adopt a flexible

approach". The authors conclude from their study that:

> … flexibility and associated manager discretion are intricate and complex notions…. In essence, … flexibility is usually only achieved by negotiation and through the building of a bank of trust rather than being seen as an entitlement or right. (p 39)

In this study, managers wanted "informality and flexibility but within some clearer structures". The study raised important questions about how far policies "can be tailored to meet the needs of individuals, how this is negotiated, and at what point managers might refuse requests from carers". The central importance of managerial discretion was a key finding, as was the recognition that the style and attitudes of managers inevitably differ. As the authors of the Keele report put it, "overt discussion and exploration of these differences may help raise awareness of carers' needs among managers and lead to greater sensitivity and equity of treatment" (p 40).

The Cambridge University Study (Dex and Scheibl, 2002)

Dex and Scheibl's study of SMEs in the East Anglian region involved face-to-face interviews with human resources or general managers in 23 SMEs (Dex and Scheibl, 2002). In half of the 23 SMEs included in the study, family-friendly employment practices had already been introduced, while in the remainder, flexible employment policies barely featured in the way the organisations were managed. The authors identified three types of SME orientation to flexible working arrangements: holistic, selective and resistant.

Holistic approaches:

> ... represented the wholehearted embrace of flexibility.... The underlying belief was that ... work–life practices were inherently good for business and good for employees.... (p 14)

In these organisations, the researchers found widespread use of 'an individual balance sheet' approach. The employer/manager valued employees for their goodwill, productivity, overtime or flexibility, and gave 'credit', in the form of a willingness to respond to employees' requests for flexibility. Key values within these organisations were: trust, openness, fairness, employee involvement and good communications. Team working and the multiskilling of individual staff was the norm within those SMEs which adopted the holistic approach.

The second type of SME orientation to flexible working arrangements was described as 'selective'. In these organisations, managers dealt pragmatically with work–life issues as they arose. In some cases this approach offered flexibility only to an 'elite' group of employees. Examples included organisations in which it was only the highly skilled professionals who organised their own time and work, and were allowed to impose their own structure on their working day. Where flexibility was allowed, it was usually supported by an explicit business case, and support for highly skilled and trained workers tended to form part of a cost-containment strategy in relation to staff retention.

In 'resistant' SMEs, there was "a marked reluctance to offer flexibility under any circumstance" (p 17). These were traditional organisations in which there was a strong belief at managerial level that introducing flexible working would bring administrative headaches and unnecessary complications for company systems. These SMEs did not recognise that their lack of flexible working practices might be contributing to organisational problems such as difficulties in recruiting staff or in retaining employees.

The authors of this report summarise the concerns about introducing flexible or family-friendly policies identified by employers and managers who were *not* using them, as relating to

- additional work and red tape from changes in the law;
- loss of clients;
- employee productivity falling;
- management finding it difficult to manage or administer the flexibility.

Some of the managers interviewed felt that "pressures for SMEs to adopt work–life practices was misplaced", in part because it did not recognise the costs they felt they would incur. Some managers reported feeling "overwhelmed with the pace of change" with which they had to cope (p 29). They perceived a business need for employees to work long hours, and believed that both their business and their client relationships would suffer if job sharing or other types of flexibility were introduced (p 30). These managers were working in very traditional organisations, and feared that flexible systems would reduce their knowledge about and control over how employees were performing their duties.

Dex and Scheibl's report acknowledges that within SMEs, certain aspects of job structure, technology, or work pressure can mitigate against the successful introduction of flexible working practices across the whole organisation – these included the low substitutability of staff with highly developed or scarce skills, long opening hours, and a high volume of work, especially work with tight delivery deadlines.

The comparative element of this study enabled the authors to test some of the arguments and rationales put forward by those SMEs which had not introduced and/or were resistant to the introduction of family-friendly practices. From this it was concluded that not all managerial attitudes accurately reflected the realities perceived by more junior workers. As the authors put it,

> Our data indicate that employers' perceptions about their employees' preferences were not entirely accurate. (p 32)

The 'client barrier' was judged to be 'not insurmountable', resistance to dividing or sharing demanding professional jobs was attributed to traditional attitudes within firms and among their clients, and it was pointed out that in other SMEs many of the operation problems affecting payroll, productivity and staff morale had been successfully overcome. The authors conclude that many of the problems perceived by employers are resolvable by:

- a change of mind set;
- management systems based on trust;
- being open to different ways of organising work and using new technology; and
- better communication between employers or managers and employees. (p 34)

The Napier, Glasgow Caledonian and Stirling University Study (Bond et al, 2002)

This study was focused exclusively on the financial services industry in Scotland (Bond et al, 2002). It drew on data from 17 companies, conducting detailed case studies in four firms, including interviews with line managers. The study found that there was a wider spread of family-friendly policies in companies that were unionised, but that smaller, non-unionised organisations had introduced a variety of relevant policies, often in an informal way and operated primarily under managerial discretion.

The case study data confirmed that although line managers had received little or no training in implementing the policies, they were expected to – and did – play a significant role in operating them. Many managers saw working time flexibility as "the essence of family-friendly working". Their decisions were influenced by issues concerning the substitutability of staff, their perceptions of what employees gave to the organisation, in terms of time and commitment, and their general attitudes towards flexible working. Above all, senior managers saw the introduction of flexible working as linked to staff retention. As one human resources manager put it:

"Current voluntary provisions are in place because of retention, not attraction. If you are flexible, you will retain people."

In all the case study companies, line managers had considerable discretion over deciding how leave arrangements and payments were implemented. Some managers expressed concern about inconsistent practice arising from this, and indicated that there were tensions between formal policy statements and informal, discretionary approaches responsive to individual employee circumstances. Managers reported that their ability to offer flexible hours of employment depended on the extent to which the role and tasks involved were time-critical, and on whether or not it was possible to substitute other workers with appropriate skills. Particular attention was drawn to the difficulty in substituting for the time of professional staff, managers, employees with specialised skills, and for individuals whose work requires 'inflexible working hours'.

As in the other studies, managers indicated that their perceptions of the performance and commitment of individual employees affected their discretionary decisions about access to the flexible and family-friendly employment policies. One manager in the study explained:

"If someone contributes well to the business, if they put in the hours for no extra pay, then that shows commitment and we'll go outside the policy for them."

The study concluded that, even within the same organisation, "family-friendly employment means different things to different people", and that informal practice was widespread. Like their employees, many managers were poorly informed about policy developments relating to work–life issues, with regard both to awareness of government policy and the law, and to internal organisational decisions. This was attributed in part to inadequate communications systems.

The study recommended that to address concerns about inconsistent policy implementation, and indeed to avoid potential legal challenges, organisations should consider:

- codifying policies;
- recording the uptake of policies;
- providing staff training about family-friendly policies and work–life balance issues, and
- testing their family-friendly policies against their equal opportunities policies.

The study conducted by Sheffield Hallam and City Universities (Yeandle et al, 2002)

This study explored employee and managerial experiences in three different sectors of employment – local government, supermarkets and retail banking – where family-friendly employment policies were being implemented (Yeandle et al, 2002). It contrasted experiences in two localities, Sheffield and Canterbury, surveying employees and interviewing managers, employed carers and care providers. It highlighted the kinds of difficulties both employees and managers experience.

The research revealed that managers had varied understanding of the policies they were responsible for implementing, and that many felt they had not received suitable training and guidance about how to implement the policies they were supposed to operate.

Managers (and employees) reported that they sometimes struggled to balance carers' needs for flexibility with service delivery considerations. Where workers could readily substitute for each other, as in supermarkets, flexible systems had been introduced with minimal disruption, but this was much more difficult where jobs were highly specialised.

It emerged that most managers were sympathetic to carers' needs. However, in the bank and the two local authorities, recent reorganisations and leaner staffing were proving barriers to effective implementation of family-friendly employment policies.

Within the organisations, managerial discretion played a crucial role in enabling carers to achieve work–life balance. This was not a locality effect (that is, local managers were not interpreting policies differently in Canterbury and Sheffield), but individual managerial discretion was critical in enabling staff with a wide range of caring responsibilities to achieve work–life balance.

The data showed that although formal organisational policies provided the framework, policy implementation occurred on an informal, flexible basis, and reflected reciprocity between managers and employees. Carers of children and dependant adults themselves reported that managerial discretion was central to achieving work–family balance and felt that managers who had care responsibilities were more sympathetic to staff needs. Managers felt obliged to balance family-friendly policies with service provision and delivery, and some expressed concerns about the potential for abuse of the flexibility offered by the policies – however, very few examples of policy abuse were cited.

Managers believed there was a business case for offering family-friendly policies, but felt there was a lack of training, guidance, consultation and communication about this policy area. They felt that service delivery targets were becoming more and more demanding, increasing pressures within their jobs. They felt this made it difficult to respond positively and flexibly to carers' circumstances.

> "We try and be as obliging as possible but it's very difficult because we need staff to serve customers, and for things like unpaid leave we don't have enough counter staff, so it's very difficult. I think we are understaffed anyway and so to let staff have more time off makes it even more difficult." (bank: manager)

> "Due to cuts we are short staffed ... if it's leave for emergency care then we just have to cope somehow, but it does increase the stress on other staff." (local authority: manager)

The study concluded that there is a need to increase awareness of formal policies, both those voluntarily introduced by senior management and those required by law, and to offer more training for managers. It was recommended that this training should address differences in managers' approaches to implementation, as these differences can result in inequities between employees. There was scant evidence of opposition to family-friendly employment policies, among managers or employees.

It can be seen from the above that the existing literature suggests a number of themes worth exploring in relation to the role played by line managers in facilitating (or obstructing) the development of work–life and family-friendly policies within organisations. Before proceeding to analysis of the detailed data from the line managers interviewed in the four projects, some of the key aspects which are discussed in the literature, but which are also reported as requiring further research and examination, are outlined.

Appendix B: Organising framework for analysis of interview data

Topics arising from interviews with line managers

1 Line manager's comments about their **own experiences of caring**

2 Line manager's comments about their **own role as a line manager**
   2a   Examples given
   2b   Difficult situations/decisions

3 Line manager's comments about **FFE policies in their organisation**
   3a   Awareness (or lack of)
   3b   Understanding
   3c   Involvement in developing FF policies
   3d   Commitment to FFE policies
   3e   How other managers operate/implement policies
   3f   Comments on reactions of staff/staff expectations

4 Line manager's **attitudes to different types of employee carers**
   4a   Parents (mothers, fathers)
   4b   Carers of older people (men/women)
   4c   Carers of disabled children (men/ women)
   4d   Carers of sick/disabled spouses (men/ women)
   4e   Carers of others

Also available from The Policy Press
Published in association with the Joseph Rowntree Foundation

Family and Work series: selected titles

Organisations, careers and counting
Rosemary Crompton, Jane Dennett and Andrea Wigfield

With the increase in mothers' employment both the government and many employers are promoting flexible working policies to improve work–life 'balance'. This report considers the effects of these changes on the lives of both women and men. It examines three employment sectors in detail – banking, grocery retail and local authorities.

Paperback £13.95 ISBN 1 86134 500 3
297 x 210mm 60 pages November 2003

Family and work in minority ethnic businesses
Anuradha Basu and Eser Altinay

While the Labour government has initiated policies to address growing concerns regarding the spillover effects of work on family life, little is known about the effects on family life of self-employment among minority ethnic groups, despite the higher incidence of self-employment among them. This report redresses this neglect by examining work–life balance issues in family-run minority ethnic businesses.

Paperback £13.95 ISBN 1 86134 548 8
297 x 210mm 52 pages November 2003

Caring and counting
The impact of mothers' employment on family relationships
Tracey Reynolds, Claire Callender and Rosalind Edwards

The main work–life balance policies promoted by government focus on the amount of time mothers spend at work. This report challenges this approach. It suggests that what happens inside the workplace and how this interacts with family life is just as important.

Paperback £14.95 ISBN 1 86134 534 8
297 x 210mm 76 pages July 2003

Combining self-employment and family life
Alice Bell and Ivana La Valle

Despite the increasing policy interest in work–life balance issues, relatively little research has been carried out into the links between self-employment and family life. This report considers, for the first time, the extent to which new family-friendly initiatives and legislation provide adequate support for self-employed parents.

Paperback £13.95 ISBN 1 86134 533 X
297 x 210mm 64 pages June 2003

Around the clock
Childcare services at atypical times
June Statham and Ann Mooney

This timely report considers how childcare services are meeting the needs of parents working atypical hours.

Paperback £11.95 ISBN 1 86134 502 X
297 x 210mm 44 pages June 2003

Geographical mobility
Family impacts
Anne E. Green and Angela Canny

This report charts the changing role and nature of geographical mobility in organisational strategies and career development. It explores the work and family life experiences of employees and partners who have faced job-related geographical mobility.

Paperback £13.95 ISBN 1 86134 466 X
297 x 210mm 68 pages May 2003

For further information about the Family and Work series and other titles published by The Policy Press, please visit our website at: **www.policypress.org.uk** or telephone +44 (0)117 331 4054

To order, please contact:
Marston Book Services • PO Box 269
Abingdon• Oxon OX14 4YN, UK
Tel: +44 (0)1235 465500
Fax: +44 (0)1235 465556
E-mail: direct.orders@marston.co.uk

JR
JOSEPH
ROWNTREE
FOUNDATION

The POLICY
P~P
PRESS